AUDUBON GUIDE
to the National Wildlife Refuges

Mid-Atlantic

AUDUBON GUIDE
to the National Wildlife Refuges

Mid-Atlantic
Delaware • Maryland • New Jersey
New York • Pennsylvania • Virginia
West Virginia

By Edward Ricciuti

Foreword by Theodore Roosevelt IV

Series Editor, David Emblidge

A Balliett & Fitzgerald Book
St. Martin's Griffin, New York

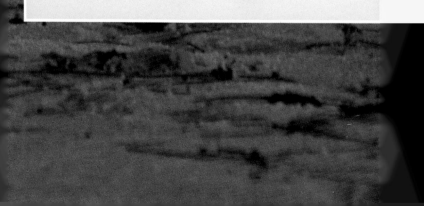

AUDUBON GUIDE TO THE NATIONAL WILDLIFE REFUGES: MID-ATLANTIC.
Copyright © 2000 by Balliett & Fitzgerald, Inc.

National Audubon Society® is a registered trademark of the National Audubon
Society, Inc.

Cartography: © Balliett & Fitzgerald, Inc. produced by Mapping Specialists Ltd.
Illustrations: Mary Sundstrom
Cover design: Michael Storrings and Sue Canavan
Interior design: Bill Cooke and Sue Canavan

Balliett & Fitzgerald Inc. Staff
Sue Canavan, Design Director
Maria Fernandez, Production Editor
Alexis Lipsitz, Executive Series Editor
Rachel Deutsch, Associate Photo Editor
Kristen Couse, Associate Editor
Paul Paddock, Carol Petino Assistant Editors
Howard Klein, Editorial Intern
Scott Prentzas, Copy Editor

Balliett & Fitzgerald Inc. would like to thank the following people for their assis-
tance in creating this series:
At National Audubon Society:
    Katherine Santone, former Director of Publishing, for sponsoring this project
    Claire Tully, Senior Vice President, Marketing
    Evan Hirsche, Director, National Wildlife Refuges Campaign
At U.S. Fish & Wildlife Service:
    Richard Coleman, former Chief, Division of Refuges, U.S. Fish & Wildlife Service
    Janet Tennyson, Outreach Coordinator
    Craig Rieben, Chief of Broadcasting & Audio Visual, U.S. Fish & Wildlife
        Service, for photo research assistance
    Pat Carrol, Chief Surveyor, U.S. Fish & Wildlife Service, for map information
    Regional External Affairs officers, at the seven U.S. Fish & Wildlife Service
        Regional Headquarters
    Elizabeth Jackson, Photographic Information Specialist, National
        Conservation Training Center, for photo research
At St. Martin's Griffin:
    Greg Cohn, who pulled it all together on his end, as well as Michael
        Storrings and Kristen Macnamara
At David Emblidge—Book Producer:
    Marcy Ross, Assistant Editor
Thanks also to Theodore Roosevelt IV and John Flicker.

ISBN 0-312-20481-7
First St. Martin's Griffin Edition: March 2000

10 9 8 7 6 5 4 3 2 1

CONTENTS

NEW YORK

PENNSYLVANIA

VIRGINIA

WEST VIRGINIA

Appendix

Foreword

America is singularly blessed in the amount and quality of land that the federal government holds in trust for its citizens. No other country can begin to match the variety of lands in our national wildlife refuges, parks and forests. From the Arctic Refuge on the North Slope of Alaska to the National Key Deer Refuge in Florida, the diversity of land in the National Wildlife Refuge (NWR) System is staggering.

Yet of all our public lands, the National Wildlife Refuge System is the least well known and does not have an established voting constituency like that of the Parks System. In part this is because of its "wildlife first" mission, which addresses the needs of wildlife species before those of people. That notwithstanding, wildlife refuges also offer remarkable opportunities for people to experience and learn about wildlife—and to have fun doing so!

The Refuge System was launched in 1903 when President Theodore Roosevelt discovered that snowy egrets and other birds were being hunted to the brink of extinction for plumes to decorate ladies' hats. He asked a colleague if there were any laws preventing the president from making a federal bird reservation out of an island in Florida's Indian River. Learning there was not, Roosevelt responded, "Very well, then I so declare it." Thus Pelican Island became the nation's first plot of land to be set aside for the protection of wildlife. Roosevelt went on to create another 50 refuges, and today there are more than 500 refuges encompassing almost 93 million acres, managed by the U.S. Fish & Wildlife Service.

The Refuge System provides critical habitat for literally thousands of mammals, birds, amphibians and reptiles, and countless varieties of plants and flowers. More than 55 refuges have been created specifically to save endangered species. Approximately 20 percent of all threatened and endangered species in the United States rely on these vital places for their survival. As a protector of our country's natural diversity, the System is unparalleled.

Setting NWR boundaries is determined, as often as possible, by the needs of species that depend on the protected lands. Conservation biology, the science that studies ecosystems as a whole, teaches us that wildlife areas must be linked by habitat "corridors" or run the risk of becoming biological islands. The resulting inability of species to transfer their genes over a wide area leaves them vulnerable to disease and natural disasters. For example, the Florida panther that lives in Big Cypress Swamp suffers from a skin fungus, a consequence, scientists believe, of inbreeding. Today's refuge managers are acutely aware of this precarious situation afflicting many species and have made protection of the System's biodiversity an important goal.

Clearly, the job of the refuge manager is not an easy one. Chronic underfunding of the System by the federal government has resulted in refuges operating with less money per employee and per acre than any other federal land-management agency. Recent efforts by some in Congress to address this shortfall have begun to show results, but the System's continued vulnerability to special interests has resulted in attempts to open refuges to oil drilling, road building in refuge wilderness areas, and military exercises.

The managers of the System have played a crucial role in responding to the limited resources available. They have created a network of volunteers who contribute tens of thousands of hours to help offset the lack of direct financing for the Refuge System. Groups like refuge "friends" and Audubon Refuge Keepers have answered the call for local citizen involvement on many refuges across the country.

I hope Americans like yourself who visit our national wildlife refuges will come away convinced of their importance, not only to wildlife but also to people. I further hope you will make your views known to Congress, becoming the voice and voting constituency the Refuge System so desperately needs.

—*Theodore Roosevelt IV*

Preface

Thank you for adding the *Audubon Guide to the National Wildlife Refuge System* to your travel library. I hope you will find this nine-volume series an indispensable guide to finding your way around the refuge system, as well as a valuable educational tool for learning more about the vital role wildlife refuges play in protecting our country's natural heritage.

It was nearly 100 years ago that Frank Chapman, an influential ornithologist, naturalist, publisher and noted Audubon member, approached President Theodore Roosevelt (as recounted by Theodore Roosevelt IV in his foreword), eventually helping to persuade him to set aside more than 50 valuable parcels of land for the protection of wildlife.

Because of limited funding available to support these new wildlife sanctuaries, Audubon stepped up and paid for wardens who diligently looked after them. And so began a century of collaboration between Audubon and the National Wildlife Refuge System. Today, Audubon chapter members can be found across the country assisting refuges with a range of projects, from viewing tower construction to bird banding.

Most recently, National Audubon renewed its commitment to the Refuge System by launching a nationwide campaign to build support for refuges locally and nationally. Audubon's Wildlife Refuge Campaign is promoting the Refuge System through on-the-ground programs such as Audubon Refuge Keepers (ARK), which builds local support groups for refuges, and Earth Stewards, a collaboration with the U.S. Fish and Wildlife Service and the National Fish and Wildlife Foundation, which uses refuges and other important bird habitats as outdoor classrooms. In addition, we are countering legislative threats to refuges in Washington, D.C., while supporting increased federal funding for this, the least funded of all federal land systems.

By teaching more people about the important role refuges play in conserving our nation's diversity of species—be they birds, mammals, amphibians, reptiles, or plants—we have an opportunity to protect for future generations our only federal lands system set aside first and foremost for wildlife conservation.

As a nation, we are at a critical juncture—do we continue to sacrifice wetlands, forests, deserts, and coastal habitat for short-term profit, or do we accept that the survival of our species is closely linked to the survival of others? The National Wildlife Refuge System is a cornerstone of America's conservation efforts. If we are to leave a lasting legacy and, indeed, ensure our future, then we must build on President Theodore Roosevelt's greatest legacy. I invite you to join us!

—*John Flicker, President, National Audubon Society*

Introduction
to the National Wildlife Refuge System

He spent entire days on horseback, traversing the landscape of domed and crumbling hills, steep forested coulees, with undulating tables of prairie above. The soft wraparound light of sunset displayed every strange contour of the Badlands and lit the colors in each desiccated layer of rock—yellow, ochre, beige, gold.

Theodore Roosevelt was an easterner. As some well-heeled easterners were wont to do, he traveled west in 1883 to play cowboy, and for the next eight years he returned as often as possible. He bought a cattle ranch, carried a rifle and a six-gun, rode a horse. North Dakota was still Dakota Territory then, but the Plains bison were about gone, down to a scattering of wild herds.

The nation faced a new and uneasy awareness of limits during Roosevelt's North Dakota years. Between 1776 and 1850, the American population had increased from 1.5 million to more than 23 million. National borders were fixed and rail and telegraph lines linked the coasts, but Manifest Destiny had a price. The ongoing plunder of wildlife threatened species such as the brown pelican and the great egret; the near-total extermination of 60 million bison loomed as a lesson many wished to avoid repeating.

Despite the damage done, the powerful landscapes of the New World had shaped the outlooks of many new Americans. From Colonial-era botanist John Bartram to 19th-century artists George Catlin and John James Audubon, naturalists and individuals of conscience explored the question of what constituted a proper human response to nature. Two figures especially, Henry David Thoreau and John Muir, created the language and ideas that would confront enduring Old World notions of nature as an oppositional, malevolent force to be harnessed and exploited. The creation in 1872 of Yellowstone as the world's first national park indicated that some Americans, including a few political leaders, were listening to what Thoreau, Muir, and these others had to say.

Roosevelt, along with his friend George Bird Grinnell, drew upon these and other writings, as well as their own richly varied experiences with nature, to take the unprecedented step of making protection of nature a social and political cause. Of his time in the Badlands, Roosevelt remarked "the romance of my life began here," and "I never would have been president if it had not been for my experiences in North Dakota." As a hunter, angler, and naturalist, Roosevelt grasped the importance of nature for human life. Though he had studied natural history as an undergraduate at Harvard, believing it would be his life's work, Roosevelt owned a passion for reform and had the will—perhaps a need—to be effective. Rather than pursuing a career as a naturalist, he went into politics. His friend George

Barren-ground caribou

New England Region
Middle Atlantic Region
Southeast Region
Northern Midwest Region
South Central Region
Southwest Region
Rocky Mountains Region
Alaska and Pacific Northwest Region
California and Hawaii Region

Migratory Flyway

G r e a t   L a k e s

New Hampshire
Vermont
Massachusetts
Maine

Minnesota

Michigan

Wisconsin

New York

Iowa

Illinois

Indiana

Ohio

Pennsylvania

Rhode Island
Connecticut
New Jersey
Delaware
Maryland

West Virginia

Virginia

Missouri

Kentucky

North Carolina

Tennessee

South Carolina

Arkansas

Mississippi

Alabama

Georgia

Atlantic Ocean

Louisiana

Florida

Puerto Rico

Gulf of Mexico

Bird Grinnell, publisher of the widely read magazine *Forest and Stream,* championed all manner of environmental protection and in 1886 founded the Audubon Society to combat the slaughter of birds for the millinery trade. Fifteen years later, TR would find himself with an even greater opportunity. In1901, when he inherited the presidency following the assassination of William McKinley, Roosevelt declared conservation a matter of federal policy.

Roosevelt backed up his words with an almost dizzying series of conservation victories. He established in 1903 a federal bird reservation on Pelican Island, Florida, as a haven for egrets, herons, and other birds sought by plume hunters. In eight years, Roosevelt authorized 150 million acres in the lower 48 states and another 85 million in Alaska to be set aside from logging under the Forest Reserve Act of 1891, compared to a total of 45 million under the three prior presidents. To these protected lands he added five national parks and 17 national monuments. The NWR system, though, is arguably TR's greatest legacy. Often using executive order to circumvent Congress, Roosevelt established 51 wildlife refuges.

The earliest federal wildlife refuges functioned as sanctuaries and little else. Visitors were rare and recreation was prohibited. Between 1905 and 1912 the first refuges for big-game species were established—Wichita Mountains in Oklahoma,

Atlantic puffins, Petit Manan NWR, Maine

the National Bison Range in Montana, and National Elk Refuge in Jackson, Wyoming. In 1924, the first refuge to include native fish was created; a corridor some 200 miles long, the Upper Mississippi National Wildlife and Fish Refuge spanned the states of Minnesota, Wisconsin, Illinois, and Iowa.

Still, the 1920s were dark years for America's wildlife. The effects of unregulated hunting, along with poor enforcement of existing laws, had decimated once-abundant species. Extinction was feared for the wood duck. Wild turkey had become scarce outside a few southern states. Pronghorn antelope, which today number perhaps a million across the West, were estimated at 25,000 or fewer. The trumpeter swan, canvasback duck, even the prolific and adaptable white-tailed deer, were scarce or extirpated across much of their historic ranges.

The Depression and Dust-bowl years, combined with the leadership of President Franklin Delano Roosevelt, gave American conservation—and the refuge system in particular—a hefty forward push. As wetlands vanished and fertile prairie soils blew away, FDR's Civilian Conservation Corps (CCC) dispatched thousands of unemployed young men to camps that stretched from Georgia to California. On the sites of many present-day refuges, they built dikes and other

Saguaro cactus and ocotillo along Charlie Bell 4WD trail, Cabeza Prieta NWR, Arizona

water-control structures, planted shelterbelts and grasses. Comprised largely of men from urban areas, the experience of nature was no doubt a powerful rediscovery of place and history for the CCC generation. The value of public lands as a haven for people, along with wildlife, was on the rise.

In 1934, Jay Norwood "Ding" Darling was instrumental in developing the federal "Duck Stamp," a kind of war bond for wetlands; hunters were required to purchase it, and anyone else who wished to support the cause of habitat acquisition could, too. Coupled with the Resettlement Act of 1935, in which the federal government bought out or condemned private land deemed unsuitable for agriculture, several million acres of homesteaded or settled lands reverted to federal ownership to become parks, national grasslands, and wildlife refuges. The Chief of the U.S. Biological Survey's Wildlife Refuge Program, J. Clark Salyer, set out on a cross-country mission to identify prime wetlands. Salyer's work added 600,000 acres to the refuge system, including Red Rock Lakes in Montana, home to a small surviving flock of trumpeter swans.

The environmental ruin of the Dust bowl also set in motion an era of government initiatives to engineer solutions to such natural events as floods, drought, and the watering of crops. Under FDR, huge regional entities such as the Tennessee Valley Authority grew, and the nation's mightiest rivers—the Columbia, Colorado, and later, the Missouri—were harnessed by dams. In the wake of these and other federal works projects, a new concept called "mitigation" appeared: If a proposed dam or highway caused the destruction of a certain number of acres of wetlands or other habitat, some amount of land nearby would be ceded to conservation in return. A good many of today's refuges were the progeny of mitigation. The federal government, like the society it represents, was on its way to becoming complex enough that the objectives of one arm could be at odds with those of another.

Citizen activism, so integral to the rise of the Audubon Society and other groups, was a driving force in the refuge system as well. Residents of rural Georgia applied relentless pressure on legislators to protect the Okefenokee Swamp. Many other refuges—San Francisco Bay, Sanibel Island, Minnesota Valley, New Jersey's Great Swamp—came about through the efforts of people with a vision of conservation close to home.

More than any other federal conservation program, refuge lands became places where a wide variety of management techniques could be tested and refined. Generally, the National Park system followed the "hands off" approach of Muir and Thoreau while the U.S. Forest Service and Bureau of Land Management, in theory, emphasized a utilitarian, "sustainable yield" value; in practice, powerful economic interests backed by often ruthless politics left watersheds, forests, and grasslands badly degraded, with far-reaching consequences for fish and wildlife. The refuge system was not immune to private enterprise—between 1939 and 1945, refuge lands were declared fair game for oil drilling, natural-gas exploration, and even for bombing practice by the U.S. Air Force—but the negative impacts have seldom reached the levels of other federal areas.

Visitor use at refuges tripled in the 1950s, rose steadily through the 1960s, and by the 1970s nearly tripled again. The 1962 Refuge Recreation Act established guidelines for recreational use where activities such as hiking, photography, boating, and camping did not interfere with conservation. With visitors came opportunities to educate, and now nature trails and auto tours, in addition to beauty, offered messages about habitats and management techniques. Public awareness of wilderness, "a place where man is only a visitor," in the words of long-time advocate Robert Marshall of the U.S. Forest Service, gained increasing social and political attention. In 1964, Congress passed the Wilderness Act, establishing guidelines for designating a host of federally owned lands as off-limits to motorized vehicles, road building, and resource exploitation. A large number of refuge lands qualified—the sun-blasted desert of Arizona's Havasu refuge, the glorious tannin-stained waters and cypress forests of Georgia's Okefenokee Swamp, and the almost incomprehensible large 8-million-acre Arctic NWR in Alaska, home to vast herds of caribou, wolf packs, and bladelike mountain peaks, the largest contiguous piece of wilderness in the refuge system.

Sachuest Point NWR, Rhode Island

Nonetheless, this was also a time of horrendous air and water degradation, with the nation at its industrial zenith and agriculture cranked up to the level of "agribusiness." A wake-up call arrived in the form of vanishing bald eagles, peregrine falcons, and osprey. The insecticide DDT, developed in 1939 and used in World War II to eradicate disease-spreading insects, had been used throughout the nation ever since, with consequences unforeseen until the 1960s. Sprayed over wetlands, streams, and crop fields, DDT had entered watersheds and from there the food chain itself. It accumulated in the bodies of fish and other aquatic life, and birds consuming fish took DDT into their systems, one effect was a calcium deficiency, resulting in eggs so fragile that female birds crushed them during incubation.

Partially submerged alligator, Anahuac NWR, Texas

Powerful government and industry leaders launched a vicious, all-out attack on the work of a marine scientist named Rachel Carson, whose book *Silent Spring*, published in 1962, warned of the global dangers associated with DDT and other biocides. For this she was labeled "not a real scientist" and "a hysterical woman." With eloquence and courage, though, Carson stood her ground. If wild species atop the food chain could be devastated, human life could be threatened, too. Americans were stunned, and demanded an immediate ban on DDT. Almost overnight, the "web of life" went from chalkboard hypothesis to reality.

Protecting imperiled species became a matter of national policy in 1973 when President Nixon signed into law the Endangered Species Act (ESA), setting guidelines by which the U.S. Fish & Wildlife Service would "list" plant and animal species as *threatened* or *endangered* and would develop a program for their recovery. Some 56 refuges, such as Ash Meadows in Nevada and Florida's Crystal River, home of the manatee, were established specifically for the protection of endangered species. Iowa's tiny Driftless Prairie refuge exists to protect the rare, beautifully colored pleistocene land snail and a wildflower, the northern monkshood. Sometimes unwieldy, forever politicized, the ESA stands as a monumental achievement. Its successes include the American alligator, bald eagle, and gray wolf. The whooping crane would almost surely be extinct today without the twin supports of ESA and the refuge system. The black-footed ferret, among the rarest mammals on earth, is today being reintroduced on a few western refuges. In 1998, nearly one-fourth of all threatened and endangered species populations find sanctuary on refuge lands.

More legislation followed. The passage of the Alaska National Interest Lands Conservation Act in 1980 added more than 50 million acres to the refuge system in Alaska.

The 1980s and '90s have brought no end of conservation challenges, faced by an increasingly diverse association of organizations and strategies. Partnerships now link the refuge system with nonprofit groups, from Ducks Unlimited and The Nature Conservancy to international efforts such as Partners in Flight, a program to monitor the decline of, and to secure habitat for, neotropical songbirds. These cooperative efforts have resulted in habitat acquisition and restoration, research, and many new refuges. Partnerships with private landowners who voluntarily offer marginally useful lands for restoration—with a sponsoring conservation group cost-sharing the project—have revived many thousands of acres of grasslands, wetlands, and riparian corridors.

Coyote on the winter range

Citizen activism is alive and well as we enter the new millennium. Protecting and promoting the growth of the NWR system is a primary campaign of the National Audubon Society, which, by the year 2000, will have grown to a membership of around 550,000. NAS itself also manages about 100 sanctuaries and nature centers across the country, with a range of opportunities for environmental education. The National Wildlife Refuge Association, a volunteer network, keeps members informed of refuge events, environmental issues, and legislative developments and helps to maintain a refuge volunteer workforce. In 1998, a remarkable 20 percent of all labor performed on the nation's refuges was carried out by volunteers, a contribution worth an estimated $14 million.

A national wildlife refuge today has many facets. Nature is ascendant and thriving, often to a shocking degree when compared with adjacent lands. Each site has its own story: a prehistory, a recent past, a present—a story of place, involving people, nature, and stewardship, sometimes displayed in Visitor Center or Headquarters exhibits, always written into the landscape. Invariably a refuge belongs to a community as well, involving area residents who visit, volunteers who log hundreds of hours, and a refuge staff who are knowledgeable and typically friendly, even outgoing, especially if the refuge is far-flung. In this respect most every refuge is a portal to local culture, be it Native American, cows and crops, or big city. There may be no better example of democracy in action than a national wildlife refuge. The worm-dunker fishes while a mountain biker pedals past. In spring, birders scan marshes and grasslands that in the fall will be walked by hunters. Compromise is the guiding principle.

What is the future of the NWR system? In Prairie City, Iowa, the Neal Smith NWR represents a significant departure from the time-honored model. Established in 1991, the site had almost nothing to "preserve." It was old farmland with scattered remnants of tallgrass prairie and degraded oak savanna. What is happening at Neal Smith, in ecological terms, has never been attempted on such a scale: the reconstruction, essentially from scratch, of a self-sustaining 8,000-acre native biome, complete with bison and elk, greater prairie chickens, and a palette of wildflowers and grasses that astonish and delight.

What is happening in human terms is equally profound. Teams of area residents, called "seed seekers," explore cemeteries, roadside ditches, and long-ignored patches of ground. Here and there they find seeds of memory, grasses and wildflowers from the ancient prairie, and harvest them; the seeds are catalogued and planted on the refuge. The expanding prairie at Neal Smith is at once new and very old. It is reshaping thousands of Iowans' sense of place, connecting them to what was, eliciting wonder for what could be. And the lessons here transcend biology. In discovering rare plants, species found only in the immediate area, people discover an identity beyond job titles and net worth. The often grueling labor of cutting brush, pulling nonnative plants, and tilling ground evokes the determined optimism of Theodore and Franklin Roosevelt and of the CCC.

As the nation runs out of wild places worthy of preservation, might large-scale restoration of damaged or abandoned lands become the next era of American conservation? There are ample social and economic justifications. The ecological justifications are endless, for, as the history of conservation and ecology has revealed, nature and humanity cannot go their separate ways. The possibilities, if not endless, remain rich for the years ahead.

—*John Grassy*

How to use this book

Local conditions and regulations on national wildlife refuges vary considerably. We provide detailed, site-specific information useful for a good refuge visit, and we note the broad consistencies throughout the NWR system (facility set-up and management, what visitors may or may not do, etc.). Contact the refuge before arriving or stop by the Visitor Center when you get there. F&W wildlife refuge managers are ready to provide friendly, savvy advice about species and habitats, plus auto, hiking, biking, or water routes that are open and passable, and public programs (such as guided walks) you may want to join.

AUDUBON GUIDES TO THE NATIONAL WILDLIFE REFUGES

This is one of nine regional volumes in a series covering the entire NWR system. **Visitable refuges**—over 300 of them—constitute about three-fifths of the NWR system. **Nonvisitable refuges** may be small (without visitor facilities), fragile (set up to protect an endangered species or threatened habitat), or new and undeveloped.

Among visitable refuges, some are more important and better developed than others. In creating this series, we have categorized refuges as A, B, or C level, with the A-level refuges getting the most attention. You will easily recognize the difference. C-level refuges, for instance, do not carry a map.

Rankings can be debated; we know that. We considered visitation statistics, accessibility, programming, facilities, and the richness of the refuges' habitats and animal life. Some refuges ranked as C-level now may develop further over time.

Many bigger NWRs have either "satellites" (with their own refuge names) separate "units" within the primary refuge or other, less significant NWRs nearby. All of these, at times, were deemed worthy of a brief mention.

ORGANIZATION OF THE BOOK

■ **REGIONAL OVERVIEW** This regional introduction is intended to give readers the big picture, touching on broad patterns in landscape formation, interconnections among plant communities, and diversity of animals. We situate NWRs in the natural world of the larger bio-region to which they belong, showing why these federally protected properties stand out as wild places worth preserving amid encroaching civilization.

We also note some wildlife management issues that will surely color the debate around campfires and

ABOUT THE U.S. FISH & WILDLIFE SERVICE Under the Department of the Interior, the U.S. Fish & Wildlife Service is the principal federal agency responsible for conserving and protecting wildlife and plants and their habitats for the benefit of the American people. The Service manages the 93-million-acre NWR system, comprised of more than 500 national wildlife refuges, thousands of small wetlands, and other special management areas. It also operates 66 national fish hatcheries, 64 U.S. Fish & Wildlife Management Assistance offices, and 78 ecological services field stations. The agency enforces federal wildlife laws, administers the Endangered Species Act, manages migratory bird populations, restores nationally significant fisheries, conserves and restores wildlife habitats such as wetlands, and helps foreign governments with their conservation efforts. It also oversees the federal-aid program that distributes hundreds of millions of dollars in excise taxes on fishing and hunting equipment to state wildlife agencies.

congressional conference tables in years ahead, while paying recognition to the NWR supporters and managers who helped make the present refuge system a reality.

■ **THE REFUGES** The refuge section of the book is organized alphabetically by state and then, within each state, by refuge name.

There are some clusters, groups, or complexes of neighboring refuges administered by one primary refuge. Some refuge complexes are alphabetized here by the name of their primary refuge, with the other refuges in the group following immediately thereafter.

■ **APPENDIX**

Nonvisitable National Wildlife Refuges: NWR properties that meet the needs of wildlife but are off-limits to all but field biologists.

Federal Recreation Fees: An overview of fees and fee passes.

Volunteer Activities: How you can lend a hand to help your local refuge or get involved in supporting the entire NWR system.

U.S. Fish & Wildlife General Information: The seven regional head-quarters of the U.S. Fish & Wildlife Service through which the National Wildlife Refuge System is administered.

National Audubon Society Wildlife Sanctuaries: A listing of the 24 National Audubon Society wildlife sanctuaries, dispersed across the U.S., which are open to the public.

Bibliography & Resources: Natural-history titles both on the region generally and its NWRs, along with a few books of inspiration about exploring the natural world.

Glossary: A listing of specialized terms (not defined in the text) tailored to this region.

Index

National Audubon Society Mission Statement

PRESENTATION OF INFORMATION: A-LEVEL REFUGE

■ **INTRODUCTION** This section attempts to evoke the essence of the place, The writer sketches the sounds or sights you might experience on the refuge, such as sandhill cranes taking off, en masse, from the marsh, filling the air with the roar of thousands of beating wings. That's a defining event for a particular refuge and a great reason to go out and see it.

■ **MAP** Some refuges are just a few acres; several, like the Alaskan behemoths, are bigger than several eastern states. The scale of the maps in this series can vary. We recommend that you also ask refuges for their detailed local maps.

■ **HISTORY** This outlines how the property came into the NWR system and what its uses were in the past.

■ **GETTING THERE** General location; seasons and hours of operation; fees, if any (see federal recreation fees in Appendix); address, telephone. Smaller or remote refuges may have their headquarters off-site. We identify highways as follows: TX14 = Texas state highway # 14; US 23 = a federal highway; I-85 = Interstate 85.

Note: Many NWRs have their own web pages at the F&W web site, http://www.fws.gov/. Some can be contacted by fax or e-mail, and if we do not provide that information here, you may find it at the F&W web site.

■ **TOURING** The **Visitor Center**, if there is one, is the place to start your tour. Some have wildlife exhibits, videos, and bookstores; others may be only a kiosk. Let someone know your itinerary before heading out on a long trail or into the backcountry, and then go explore.

Most refuges have roads open to the public; many offer a wildlife **auto tour,** with wildlife information signs posted en route or a brochure or audiocassette to guide you. Your car serves as a bird blind if you park and remain quiet. Some refuge roads require 4-wheel-drive or a high-chassis vehicle. Some roads are closed seasonally to protect habitats during nesting seasons or after heavy rain or snow.

Touring also covers **walking and hiking** (see more trail details under ACTIV-ITIES) and **biking.** Many refuge roads are rough; mountain or hybrid bikes are more appropriate than road bikes. When water is navigable, we note what kinds of **boats** may be used and where there are boat launches.

■ **WHAT TO SEE**

Landscape and climate: This section covers geology, topography, and climate: primal forces and raw materials that shaped the habitats that lured species to the refuge. It also includes weather information for visitors.

Plant life: This is a sampling of noteworthy plants on the refuge, usually sorted by habitat, using standard botanical nomenclature. Green plants bordering watery places are in "Riparian Zones"; dwarfed trees, shrubs, and flowers on windswept mountaintops are in the "Alpine Forest"; and so forth.

Wildflowers abound, and you may want to see them in bloom. We give advice about timing your visit, but ask the refuge for more. If botany and habitat relationships are new to you, you can soon learn to read the landscape as a set of interrelated communities. Take a guided nature walk to begin.

(Note: In two volumes, "Plants" is called "Habitats and Plant Communities.")

Animal life: The national map on pages 4 and 5 shows the major North American "flyways." Many NWRs cluster in watery territory underneath the birds' aerial superhighways. There are many birds in this book, worth seeing simply for their beauty. But ponder, too, what birds eat (fish, insects, aquatic plants), or how one species (the mouse) attracts another (the fox), and so on up the food chain, and you'll soon understand the rich interdependence on display in many refuges.

Animals use camouflage and stealth for protection; many are nocturnal. You may want to come out early or late to increase your chances of spotting them. Refuge managers can offer advice on sighting or tracking animals.

Grizzly bears, venomous snakes, alligators, and crocodiles can indeed be dangerous. Newcomers to these animals' habitats should speak with refuge staff about precautions before proceeding.

■ **ACTIVITIES** Some refuges function not only as wildlife preserves but also as recreation parks. Visit a beach, take a bike ride, and camp overnight, or devote your time to serious wildlife observation.

Camping and swimming: If not permissible on the refuge, there may be federal or state campgrounds nearby; we mention some of them. Planning an NWR camping trip should start with a call to refuge headquarters.

Wildlife observation: This subsection touches on strategies for finding species most people want to see. Crowds do not mix well with certain species; you

---

A NOTE ON HUNTING AND FISHING Opinions on hunting and fishing on federally owned wildlife preserves range from "Let's have none of it" to "We need it as part of the refuge management plan." The F&W Service follows the latter approach, with about 290 hunting programs and 260 fishing programs. If you have strong opinions on this topic, talk with refuge managers to gain some insight into F&W's rationale. You can also write to your representative or your senators in Washington.

For most refuges, we summarize the highlights of the hunting and fishing options. You must first have required state and local licenses for hunting or fishing. Then you must check with refuge headquarters about special restrictions that may apply on the refuge; refuge bag limits, for example, or duration of season may be different from regulations elsewhere in the same state.

Hunting and fishing options change from year to year on many refuges, based on the size of the herd or of the flock of migrating birds. These changes may reflect local weather (a hard winter trims the herd) or disease, or factors in distant habitats where animals summer or winter. We suggest what the options usually are on a given refuge (e.g., some birds, some mammals, fish, but not all etc..). It's the responsibility of those who wish to hunt and fish to confirm current information with refuge headquarters and to abide by current rules.

COMMON SENSE, WORTH REPEATING

Leave no trace Every visitor deserves a chance to see the refuge in its pristine state. We all share the responsibility to minimize our impact on the landscape. "Take only pictures and leave only footprints," and even there you'll want to avoid trampling plant life by staying on established trails. Pack out whatever you pack in. Ask refuge managers for guidance on low-impact hiking and camping.

Respect private property Many refuges consist of noncontiguous parcels of land, with private properties abutting refuge lands. Respect all Private Property and No Trespassing signs, especially in areas where native peoples live within refuge territory and hunt or fish on their own land.

Water Protect the water supply. Don't wash dishes or dispose of human waste within 200 ft. of any water. Treat all water for drinking with iodine tablets, backpacker's water filter, or boiling. Clear water you think is OK may be contaminated upstream by wildlife you cannot see.

may need to go away from established observation platforms to have success. Learn a bit about an animal's habits, where it hunts or sleeps, what time of day it moves about. Adjust your expectations to match the creature's behavior, and your chances of success will improve.

Photography: This section outlines good places or times to see certain species. If you have a zoom lens, use it. Sit still, be quiet, and hide yourself. Don't approach the wildlife; let it approach you. Never feed animals or pick growing plants.

Hikes and walks: Here we list specific outings, with mileages and trailhead locations. Smooth trails and boardwalks, suitable for people with disabilities, are noted. On bigger refuges, there may be many trails. Ask for a local map. If you go bushwacking, first make sure this is permissible. Always carry a map and compass.

Seasonal events: National Wildlife Refuge Week, in October, is widely celebrated, with guided walks, lectures, demonstrations, and activities of special interest to children. Call your local refuge for particulars. At other times of the year there are fishing derbies, festivals celebrating the return of migrating birds, and other events linked to the natural world. Increasingly, refuges post event schedules on their web pages.

Publications: Many NWR brochures are free, such as bird and wildflower checklists. Some refuges have pamphlets and books for sale, describing local habitats and species.

Note: The categories of information above appear in A and B refuges in this book; on C-level refuges, options are fewer, and some of these headings may not appear.

—*David Emblidge*

Mid-Atlantic

A Regional Overview

Small, fleeting forms, silvered by moonlight, rocket through the star-speckled sky of a May night. Vast multitudes of shorebirds, millions of them, driven by instinct's iron rule, fly at breakneck speed away from South America, a wintering haven that is now far behind them. The sun is edging northward, carrying warmth that greens marshes, meadows, woodlands, and, eventually, the Arctic tundra on which these small birds breed. And so, the shorebirds hurtle north, following their star, jetting toward the rim of Arctic seas. The land on which they will nest is still in the frigid grasp of cold but is slowly cooking up the ingredients of a warm welcome to greet them when they eventually arrive.

Some of these small, long-billed birds—many species are smaller than a robin—have flown for 5,000 miles, stopping but once on the way, with thousands of miles yet to go before journey's end. Hunger gnaws at them. Their energy reserves have been drained by their marathon trek. Their flight may be headlong but it is not precipitous. An internal guidance system, designed by nature and not fully fathomed by humans, unerringly directs them toward a precise target, a rest area, if you will, that will provide a respite before they continue their journey. Unerringly, they home in on the long, sandy beaches and tidal marshes that are the salient natural features of the Middle Atlantic coast. On these shores, especially those of Delaware Bay, they will rest their tired wings for two weeks or so, while busily fueling up on the abundant marsh plants, before resuming their migration to the far North.

Most of the national wildlife refuges in the Middle Atlantic states—defined here as New York, New Jersey, Pennsylvania, Delaware, Maryland, Virginia, and West Virginia—were established primarily to preserve habitat for migratory birds, especially aquatic species, such as shorebirds and waterfowl, as well as neotropical songbirds. Many such birds follow the Atlantic coast on seasonal migrations, using a corridor called the Atlantic Flyway. Some of them are transient in the Middle Atlantic, while others winter or nest there. Either way, the refuges help provide habitat essential to their survival.

The natural wealth these refuges sustain is shared by a host of other organisms. From the endangered Delmarva fox squirrel to the imperiled pine barrens tree frog, distinguished by an exquisite lavender eye stripe; from red-barked Atlantic cedars to pitcher plants, which feast on insects, the species the Middle Atlantic refuges help conserve are exceedingly diverse.

A few Middle Atlantic refuges—Great Dismal Swamp in Virginia, for example—are true wildernesses. But others, including the Edwin B. Forsythe refuge in southern New Jersey, lie literally within sight of panoramas that people, not nature, have created: towers of steel, concrete, and glass rising toward the heavens in imitation of a mountainous skyline.

Cattle egret, Edwin B. Forsythe NWR, New Jersey

Perhaps it is these refuges, at the margins of or even within the urban realm, that are the

MID-ATLANTIC

DELAWARE
1 Bombay Hook NWR
2 Prime Hook NWR

MARYLAND
3 Blackwater NWR
4 Eastern Neck NWR
5 Patuxent Research Refuge

NEW JERSEY
6 Cape May NWR
7 Edwin B. Forsythe NWR
8 Great Swamp NWR
9 Wallkill NWR

NEW YORK
10 Iroquois NWR
11 Montezuma NWR
12 Wertheim NWR

PENNSYLVANIA
13 Erie NWR
14 John Heinz NWR at Tinicum

VIRGINIA
15 Back Bay NWR
16 Chincoteague NWR
17 Eastern Shore of Virginia NWR
18 Great Dismal Swamp NWR
19 Mason Neck NWR
20 Occoquan Bay NWR
21 Presquile NWR

WEST VIRGINIA
22 Canaan Valley NWR
23 Ohio River Islands NWR

Lake Erie

Erie

13

Pittsburgh

Wheeling

23

22

West Virginia

Huntington

★Charleston

most important of all, for they remind urban America of the natural world from which it evolved.

This book covers national wildlife refuges—some actually complexes of very small refuges—accessible to the public, although the extent of visitor facilities varies. Most of these refuges contain a core of aquatic environments, whether wetlands, streams, ponds, or coastline. Some of them are hundreds of miles inland: Montezuma NWR in central New York, for instance. The majority, however, are by or near the sea.

GEOLOGY

Fronted by the sea, the Middle Atlantic is backed by mountains, principally the great ridges and verdant valleys of the Appalachian Chain. Although separated by hundreds of miles, mountains and sea are inextricably linked by the water cycle. Rain and snow that water the mountains flow from the mountains in streams large and small. The water crosses the Piedmont, the hilly region between the interior peaks and the Middle Atlantic Coastal Plain. At the eastern edge of the Piedmont, streams plunge over the fall line, where rough water and waterfalls blocked early colonists from navigating waterways farther inland. Once on the coastal plain, which at most is no more than 300 feet above sea level and at least just a few feet, the streams become languid and ease their way to the ocean.

It might be said that, geologically, the mountains are the primal soul of the Middle Atlantic, while the coastal plain is young at heart. Trying to date precisely the birth of a mountain chain can be as problematic as counting angels on a pinhead, but geologists generally agree that the Appalachians have roots that go back 500 million years.

Colliding continental plates in the earth's crust shoved aside rocks and created a trough, which was filled by a broad sea. Over the course of 300 million years, sediments were deposited on the sea bottom, which slowly sank under their weight, allowing additional sediments to accumulate, to a depth of 40,000 feet in places. Then, about 180 million years ago, the rock formed by the ancient sediment was thrust and folded upward into the precursor of the modern Appalachians. Time wore these mountains down into an immense plain. But the mountains eventually were reborn as the earth's crust warped upward. Time again took a hand to these upstart mountains and gentled the once-craggy face of their peaks. Rivers—the Delaware, Susquehanna, and Potomac—cut through the mountain ridges, forming valleys that now bear their names.

From our point of view, the mountains appear to stand fast. But time continues to humble them, imperceptibly but relentlessly, eroding a grain or rock here, another there, so that the heights eventually will be brought low. The visage of the Appalachians and associated mountains is aged. Countless millions of years from now, however, if the crust of the earth again heaves upward, the face of the landscape will be refashioned once more.

The terrain of the coastal plain, where these rivers empty into the sea, is, geologically speaking, a toddler. Twelve thousand years ago, before the last glaciers retreated and sea levels began to rise, the plain extended some 200 miles seaward of its present shoreline. The plain and the continental shelf are parts of the same package, only nowadays the shelf is under water. Just as a growing child's face increasingly takes on mature features, that of the coastal plain is changing as the sea continues to encroach upon the land. The water level in Chesapeake Bay, the drowned valley of the Susquehanna River, marches inland at about a foot per century. That may seem slow going, but consider this: Some marshes

Moonrise over saltwater marsh, Chincoteague NWR, Virginia

at the Blackwater NWR on the Eastern Shore of Maryland are filling up and evolving into ponds as the sea creeps up the land. Similarly, the barrier islands of sand that edge the coast, protecting tidal marshes and bays behind them, are inching westward as sea level rises.

By virtue of its name alone, the Middle Atlantic is tied to the sea. All but two states in the region front the ocean. Pennsylvania does not, but the Delaware River at Philadelphia throbs to the beat of the tides and is only some 60 miles from the beaches of South Jersey. West Virginia? It is a maverick among states, in ways sociological as well as geographical, and many of its citizens are proud of the fact. Yet, by virtue of its latitude and the fact that, until the Civil War era it was part of Virginia, West Virginia is Middle Atlantic, although many a Mountaineer might take issue with the statement.

CLIMATE

Because the Middle Atlantic stretches from the mountains to the sea and from the Canadian border of New York State to the margins of the southeastern states, its

Wetlands, Iroquois NWR, New York

climate is relatively varied. Winters in upper New York State, especially in the Adirondacks but also in central New York, are often brutal, with heavy snows and temperatures dropping far below zero. The heights of the Appalachians extend a finger of northern climate to the southern border of the region, and in winter they can be laden with several feet of snow, intercepted by the peaks from storms blowing eastward. The climate moderates east of the mountains, a function of gradually descending altitude and proximity to the sea. While the growing season in the extreme north is less than five months, that of the Piedmont can be six, and additional weeks are tacked on along the coastal plain.

The climate maker of the coast is the ocean. During the summer, the ocean soaks up the sun's heat, although there is plenty of warmth remaining to make days hot and sticky. In winter, the sea is like a slow-burning furnace, releasing its stored heat gently, sparing the plain from the snows that fall inland, if not from rain. The Gulf Stream, carrying tropical water from the Gulf of Mexico over the continental shelf northward along the East Coast as far as Cape Cod, adds to the sea's moderating effect.

The Middle Atlantic has abundant, but not excessive, rainfall. Between 40 and 50 inches a year is the norm in many places, and that is easily sufficient to support the growth of forests, some of them lush.

HABITATS AND PLANT LIFE

The plant communities of the Middle Atlantic reflect not only available moisture but also altitude, latitude, and, in cases, the impact of the sea. Much of New York and Pennsylvania is dominated by what is known as transition forest, a mix of deciduous trees, which rule farther south, and conifers, which extend from the boreal forest of Canada, the Great North Woods. Transition forest and even a thin crest of the boreal extend southward along the colder heights of the Appalachians.

The mixed deciduous forest, with its oaks, maples, and hickories, is your typical eastern forest. In the Middle Atlantic, its heart is east of the mountains, west of the coastal plain, although it has outliers aplenty in either direction. The mixed forest, by and large, is relatively young, some of it less than a century old. Virtually all of the original forest was cleared for agriculture or industry during the 18th and early 19th centuries. With diminished agriculture—there still are many farms in places like southern Delaware and eastern Maryland—trees have returned. The coastal plain—at times land, at times continental shelf, over the course of eons—is the realm of pines: loblolly and Virginia in the south, pitch pine and short-leaf in the north. Often mixing with the pines are scraggly oaks, including chestnut and blackjack oaks. The pines thrive in soils that are neither moist nor fertile enough to support great stands of deciduous trees. The earth beneath one's feet on the coastal plain is sandy, a product of rising and falling seas and of sediment, washed south after the northern glaciers retreated. This is thin soil, a spendthrift when it comes to storing moisture and, as a result, impoverished of nutrients.

Biologically richer than the most fertile forest and indeed one of the most fecund plant communities on earth is the thin green line of salt marshes that rims the estuaries and backwaters, often behind barrier islands, of the Middle Atlantic. There, the growth and decay of plants, particularly the salt-tolerant cordgrasses, are cooked by microorganisms into a nourishing soup that enriches the sea. Flushed by the tides, the seaside marshes are factories of bio-organic matter. They are the homes of crabs and other invertebrates, as well as nurseries for fish and feeding grounds for birds. It is not by coincidence that many of the major national wildlife refuges of the Middle Atlantic have been created around these saline and brackish marshes that, depending on the time of day, straddle the line between land and sea.

WILDLIFE

Overall, the mammals of the Middle Atlantic, large and small, are typical of those inhabiting the eastern half of the country: beaver and mink, muskrats and eastern moles. And white-tailed deer, lots of them. But, oddly, if there is a mammal

Northern pintails

White-tailed deer, Wertheim NWR, New York

that can be said to represent the region, it is a marsupial, the only pouched mammal in the United States. Its common name bears the flag of the Middle Atlantic: Virginia opossum.

When it comes to birds of the Middle Atlantic, waterbirds—ducks, geese, shorebirds, and wading birds—are a given, as long as their feeding and resting habitats are preserved. But, with controls on such pesticides as DDT and wildlife conservation efforts that began in the 1960s, the Middle Atlantic has become a citadel for many birds of prey, including those, such as the American bald eagle and the peregrine falcon, that were on the verge of extinction but have now recovered. At refuges such as Montezuma in New York and Mason Neck in Virginia, American bald eagles soar in the skies and roost on tall trees. Peregrine falcons, a few decades ago nearly extinct, now rocket over New Jersey's Cape May and can be seen by visitors to the Edwin B. Forsythe refuge, where they nest. Ospreys, also vanishing not so many years ago, circle the skies again and take advantage of nesting platforms constructed on wildlife refuges and other lands.

Lost in the shuffle of species sought by birders but esteemed by hunters is an upland shorebird, the American woodcock—distinct from its European cousin. Nesting largely in the north, it migrates southward during the fall, flying most actively when the moon is full. Declining for various reasons, including perhaps loss of breeding habitat in the north, the woodcock, with its long, upturned bill adapted to probing moist soil for earthworms, nestles in by the thousands in southern New Jersey during its fall migration. The Cape May refuge has become one of the woodcock's key stopping places before it takes off on the voyage across Delaware Bay.

Urban areas of the Middle Atlantic are seeing a remarkable resurgence of wildlife traditionally associated with rural areas. Striped skunks, raccoons, and gray squirrels have always been fixtures of the citified environment as well as that of the hinterlands. But now certain large creatures have taken a cue, especially species like the white-tailed deer, which have demonstrated a remarkable ability to adapt to human activities. Many of these animals spill over from nearby lands that are reservations for wild animals. White-tailed deer, for example, like to feed in both forest and field and especially on the edge, or interface, between them. They are nippers, loving to browse on the tender shoots of growing plants. The clearing of forests during the last century and conversion of woodlands into treeless agricultural fields contributed to a precipitous decline in deer herds. Later, as hardscrabble farms were abandoned, woodland reemerged. Young woodlands and abandoned fields provided plentiful browse for deer, so the whitetail population recovered. The farmlands that still prosper in places such as Delaware and Pennsylvania are now edged by woodlands, so deer prosper in these areas, although sometimes their feeding habits threaten the prosperity of farmers. Encouraged, state wildlife agencies have emphasized management of deer habitat.

Enter the suburbs. Lawns and shrubs, bordered by trees, are a human-made replica of the forest-field interface. Such habitat is perfect for whitetails, especially since it contains few natural predators. Given cheek-by-jowl housing development, most suburban areas do not allow hunting to reduce the deer population. Some municipalities, driven by complaints about ravished gardens and, in many cases, fear of the deer tick that carries Lyme disease, have hired professional deer shooters, with small-caliber rifles, to reduce the herds by night.

The coyotes help. They arrived in northern New England from the west about 50 years ago—some scientists believed that they interbred with Canadian wolves along the way—and have filtered down into several Middle Atlantic states. Coyotes will occasionally kill deer, mostly those that are sick or injured, weeding out the unfit and the infirm from the herd.

White-tailed deer and coyotes have learned to live among dense human populations, even on the margins of major cities. So, although to a lesser degree, have black bears, which are increasing in some northern areas and occasionally turn up in New York and New Jersey suburbs. Of course, the interaction between people and creatures such as deer and bears—coyotes, apparently, go where they will—stems not only from the fact that these animals are infiltrating. To take a phrase from Bambi, "*Man* is in the forest." Suburban sprawl brings increasing numbers of people right to the edge of habitat these animals call home.

It is ironic that large species such as these seem to be increasing in urban and suburban areas, while some small creatures, which might appear well qualified to live amid human activities, are in trouble. One is the Delmarva fox squirrel, which on the surface may seem to have habitat needs similar to those of the slightly smaller gray squirrel, so common in cities that it is sometimes called the "tree rat." But the fox squirrel is apparently more dependent on mature forest, especially forests with abundant oaks and hickories, than its gray cousin. Fragmentation of its Delmarva Peninsula habitat by agriculture—and in some cases, replacement of deciduous forest with pines—has endangered this small creature. Its chief strongholds are found on national wildlife refuges, such as Blackwater and Prime Hook.

From mountains to sea, the wildlife of the Middle Atlantic is as varied and splendid as that of any other place on earth. It will remain so, if humans allow.

THEN AND NOW

They were the first ones. The hunters, with their fluted points of stone, trekked into the Middle Atlantic from west and south, as northern glaciers retreated. When they first arrived is hard to tell. But their weapon points of chalcedony and flint—long, pointed, and sharp-edged—suggest they hunted Ice Age big game, perhaps shaggy mammoths and prehistoric bison with horns 6 feet across, tip to tip. They were supreme hunters, following their quarry even—it is assumed—out on to the then-dry expanses of the continental shelf.

The Ice Ages have ended. Conifers retreat to the north and the deciduous forest replaces them. Sea levels rise. The ancestors of present-day Native Americans turn from the biggest game to game, like deer, still large but not sizable enough to feed the entire band for long. And there are other sources of food: rabbits, squirrels, waterfowl, nuts from the broad-leaved trees, berries from plants that have found a home in the wake of the retreating cold. Moreover, the beaches are no longer far away. Finfish and shellfish are there for the taking.

The small groups of ancient peoples of North America gave rise to the Native American tribes encountered by European colonists. Their names, some bestowed upon them by the newcomers, were eventually linked to rivers, lakes, and other natural features of the land—Cayuga, Mohawk, Susquehanna, Erie, Huron, and Delaware, for example.

Contrary to popular belief, Native Americans did have an impact on the environment, for worse as well as better. They slaughtered the Ice Age bison and other big game, hastening their extinction, although the retreat of the glaciers was the true killing blow. They set fires on the plains, which kept the country open, so that prairie flowers, grasses, and modern bison could thrive. Still, nature as a whole was relatively undisturbed by Native Americans.

Once Euro-Americans began to colonize the continent, however, the rules changed. The Middle Atlantic was one of the first areas to feel the brunt of settlement and, later, of industrialization. Forests vanished, as did the animals inhabiting them; as early as the 1790s, the last wood bison in Pennsylvania perished, for example.

We all know the story. Progress, however one defines it, has its price, a costly one in terms of salt marshes drained and sand dunes destroyed by beachfront development; of rivers and lakes polluted and ancient oaks and hemlocks felled. Be that as it may, today there is progress of another sort. Much of what humans have done harmfully to the environment they can undo. And part of the way the wrongs can be righted lies in the establishment and careful management of the federal system of national wildlife refuges.

GETTING UNDER WAY

The first NWRs were established as a holding action, to preserve wildlife habitat that was drastically declining. Some new refuges are still created to preserve islands of nature amidst a flood of development. The U.S. Fish & Wildlife Service, managers of the NWR System, take a proactive stance. Many mid-Atlantic refuges are epicenters of action, and that includes cooperative efforts with state agencies and conservation organizations, to expand and enhance the natural world.

Refuges, such as Bombay Hook and Prime Hook (Delaware) and Cape May (New Jersey), are in the forefront of this movement in the Middle Atlantic. These three are included in the 126,000 acres of Delaware Bay wetlands, at the 70 sites on both sides of the bay in New Jersey and Delaware, that were singled out in 1992 as a Wetland of International Importance. The designation was made under the RAMSAR Convention on Wetlands, agreed to by most of the world's nations at Ramsar, Iran, in 1971. International recognition gives Middle Atlantic conservation considerable clout. At the NWRs themselves, although sometimes strained by underfunding and understaffing, there is research and, importantly, public education programs, formal and informal. Meanwhile, many refuges, even the senior citizens among them, are still trying to grow, seeking funds and agreements that will extend their boundaries. It is working. Half of the coastline in the Delaware side of Delaware Bay is in the hands of the federal and state governments. Even so, it is not fully protected. Delaware Bay is the largest port of entry for oil on the East Coast. The consequences of a major oil spill there could have a horrendous impact not only on local wildlife but on the legions of birds that migrate between the two Americas, enriching the fauna of each continent.

The birds know nothing of oil tankers, nor of the petroleum that drives the modern world. They come to the shores, as they have since the glacial ice retreated, unknowingly relying on the largesse they find there. In the refuges, you can see them, along with their fellows in nature: the warblers, the muskrats, the deer, the beavers, and the otter. And when you watch them, think of this paraphrase of a prayer, uttered at a funer-

Canada goose, Edwin B. Forsythe NWR, New Jersey

al for an old woods walker: "May the woodcock always fly on the full moon, and may grouse forever drum in the green spring woods." That is why these refuges are there; so that you may never have to live in a world without the whir of feathered wings.

Bombay Hook NWR
Smyrna, Delaware

Boardwalk overlook, Bombay Hook NWR

The snows come early to Bombay Hook in the October sun, when a blizzard of white descends upon the marshes on the western shore of Delaware Bay. Up to 200,000 snow geese, their calls filling the air like raucous laughter, settle in to rest and gorge on the marshland vegetation on their journey south from breeding grounds on the arctic tundra. As snow-white as their name implies, save for brilliant jet-black wingtips, the snow geese have fellow travelers on their exodus from the north. Some years, more than 50,000 migrant ducks blanket the Bombay Hook marshes as they dabble and dip for food.

Fall is not the only season for epic wildlife gatherings at Bombay Hook, testifying to the resiliency and fecundity of nature. In May, when the cordgrass in the salt marshes and the wild rice in the freshwater wetlands experience the flush of spring growth, two other hosts arrive, one from the air, the other from the sea. It is no coincidence that a million shorebirds, beating north from as far away as Argentina, and a million horseshoe crabs, emerging from the water, arrive explosively on the beaches of Delaware Bay each May. The crabs come ashore to spawn, the females depositing their dull-green eggs in the sand. The birds, after a nonstop flight, arrive to refuel before continuing north to their own breeding grounds on the tundra. The bulk of the food that provides energy for the rest of their journey? Those tiny, green just-laid eggs, courtesy of the horseshoe crab.

HISTORY

Native Americans called it Canaresse: "at the thickets." After a Dutch settler purchased the land from the natives, it became known as *Bompies Hoeck,* meaning "little tree point." Over time, the Dutch name became the more Anglicized "Bombay Hook." There were indeed plenty of trees at Bombay Hook in Colonial times, but they are gone, casualties of raging sea storms. Covering about 16,000 acres, the refuge is 80 percent salt marsh, with around 3,000 acres of freshwater impoundments, forested uplands, and croplands split down the middle. Bombay Hook NWR was established with considerable foresight in 1937 as a resting and feeding area for migratory and wintering waterfowl, as well as other migratory birds. Today, it is a relative island of marshland amid a heavily developed coastline.

GETTING THERE

From the south, take Rte. 13 from Dover, then Rte. 42 east to Rte. 9, Leipsic. Go north for 2 mi. on Rte. 9 to Whitehall Neck Rd., ending at the refuge entrance. From the north, take Rte. 13 from Smyrna, then go east on Rte. 12 for 5 mi. to Rte. 9. After 0.25 mi., turn left on Whitehall Neck Rd.

■ **SEASON:** Refuge open year-round.

■ **HOURS:** General refuge: sunrise to sunset. Visitor Center open weekdays 8 a.m.–4 p.m., weekends 9 a.m.–5 p.m., March–May, Sept.–Dec.

■ **FEES:** Entrance fee $4 per vehicle. Golden Passes and Federal Duck Stamps Accepted.

■ **ADDRESS:** Bombay Hook NWR, 2591 Whitehall Neck Rd., Smyrna, DE 19977

■ **TELEPHONE:** 302/653-9345

TOURING BOMBAY HOOK

■ **BY AUTOMOBILE:** The auto-tour route meanders along the fringes of tidal marsh and freshwater impoundments and through woodlands. Leaving the vehicle is allowed.

■ **BY FOOT:** Five hiking trails, a quarter-mile to a mile long, include a boardwalk into the salt marsh. The trails are Bear Swamp, Parson Point, and Boardwalk. Parson Point Trail is closed from Dec. to June to protect the privacy of a pair of bald eagles that nest nearby. The auto-tour route, 12 miles long, is also open to walkers.

■ **BY BICYCLE:** Bikes are permitted on the auto-tour route.

■ **BY CANOE, KAYAK, OR BOAT:** Boating is not allowed within refuge boundaries.

WHAT TO SEE

■ **LANDSCAPE AND CLIMATE** Flat as a platter, Bombay Hook lies low to the sea, with virtually no part of the refuge more than 10 feet above sea level. This is a gentle terrain, bounded by Delaware Bay and vast agricultural fields of grain, emerald green in spring and dotted with elegant farmhouses in the Queen Anne style, bespeaking prosperity that comes from the soil. On sultry summer days thunderstorms may rumble in the sky, but storms can roll in from the bay at any season. Heat and humidity are taxing here in summer. Bombay Hook's fierce-biting greenhead flies and mosquitoes terrorize explorers of wood and marsh. People may find the depths of winter dreary here, but wildlife thrive in the chilly seasons. A pair of bald eagles, which breed intermittently on the refuge, begin refurbishing their nest in January. Pintail ducks begin arriving in February. Spring and autumn weather bring the best of the refuge's wildlife spectaculars.

■ PLANT LIFE

Tidal marsh The largest plant community of Bombay Hook is its salt marshes, comprising three-quarters of the refuge's acreage. Other than Boardwalk Trail, visitors have little or no chance at close-up exploration of the vast morass, vegetated mostly by salt-marsh cordgrass, extending seaward from Bombay Hook's uplands

BOMBAY HOOK NWR

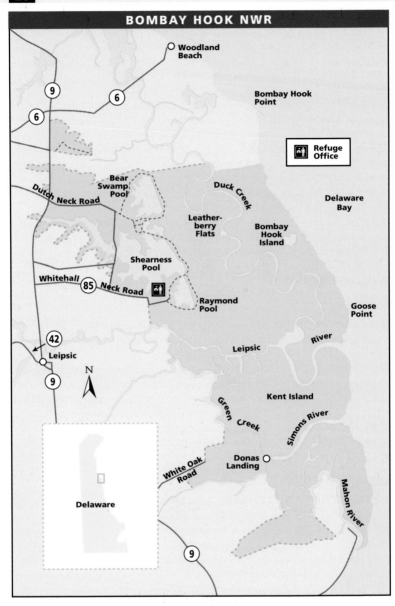

as far as the eye can see. It is probably just as well. Salt marshes are easy going for muskrats—the mounds of mud and reeds that are their dens dot the marsh—but not for people. The muck sucks at feet, then at knees; concealed tidal creeks invite a soggy, even dangerous, fall. Salt marshes are fragile places, despite their resistance to ravages of wind, water, and extreme temperatures.

To the casual glance, there is a monotony to the cordgrass that dominates the salt marsh. But it is truly a marvel. Along mangrove trees living farther south in similar habitats, cordgrass is among the few green plants that tolerate water of high salinity. The secret is its ability to eliminate salt absorbed from seawater. Salt exits through the leaves, appearing as crystals, almost too small for the human eye to see.

Brackish marsh Best viewed from Boardwalk Trail, brackish-water habitats at Bombay Hook contain a mix of plants from freshwater and saltwater habitats. Here are stands of saltmeadow cordgrass—it is harvested in some places and sold as garden mulch—which grows on higher ground than its salt-marsh cousin. Mixed with the cordgrass is the three-square bulrush, a tall wetlands plant found in transition zones between the realms of freshwater and saltwater. Along the trail are persimmon trees, with bark as rough as alligator skin, and orange fruits that are a favorite food of many animals (as reflected in the old southern folk song "Possum Up a Simmon Tree").

Freshwater impoundments The auto tour winds around four impoundments: Shearness Pool, Bear Swamp Pool, Raymond Pool, and Finis Pool. These pools range from open marsh to woody swamp, offering some of the best wildlife viewing from the auto tour. Their waters support typical freshwater marsh and pond plants: cattails, water lilies, and pondweed.

Woodlands Woodlands occupy only a small fraction of Bombay Hook; the auto tour and some of the trails wind through them. The woodlands are relatively open, with tulip trees, trunks straight as telephone poles, rising toward the sky amid stands of oaks, hickories, and sweet gum trees. Sweet gum seeds are enclosed in spiny pods called "monkey balls" that litter the ground in spring. Sweet gum, which can be seen along Bear Swamp Trail, marks an early stage in the succession of old fields into mature forest oaks, hickories, and tulip trees, evident toward the end of the auto tour. In moist areas of the forest, ferns such as bracken and royal, and the hooded flowers of jack-in-the-pulpit, lend grace to the woodland floor. In spring, the woodland corridors echo to the busy calls of warblers and the symphony of other songbird melodies.

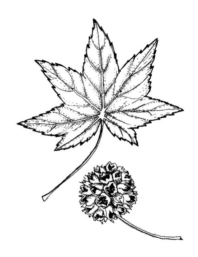

Sweet gum leaf and seedpod

ANIMAL LIFE Spectacular animal events are here, no question. Snow geese arrive in hordes. Squadrons of shorebirds rocket toward the mudflats in flocks that twist and turn with balletic precision. But there are plenty of other, more subtle vignettes of nature to be observed at Bombay Hook. A northern water snake basks on the auto trail (one reason speed limits should be observed); a pile of painted turtles suns on a log in Finis Pool; a red-bellied woodpecker *"churrrs"* in the woods.

Birds About 300 species of birds have been spotted at Bombay Hook, but you will probably never see them all. Royal terns occasionally visit the refuge in spring and fall. Black rails are here in every season except winter but stay very well camouflaged. No matter. You will find birds galore at Bombay Hook, especially during the spring and autumn. October and November are the prime months for waterfowl.

A waterfowl bonus in fall is the regal tundra swan. The masses of shorebirds—including semipalmated sandpipers, dunlins, and willets—peak during the last

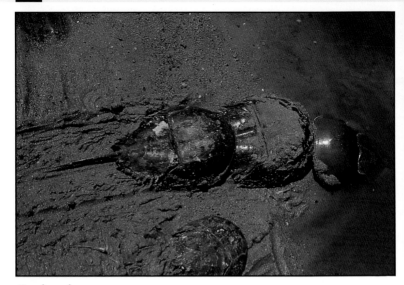

Horseshoe crabs

two weeks of May. Many of these probers of beach and mudflat also pass through in late summer and early fall, clad in their relatively drab winter colors. May is migrating warbler time, as these small woodland birds journey north, clad in brilliant breeding plumage; fall brings them back on the way south, their colors muted.

Along the auto tour, alongside Shearness Pool, try out the spotting scope. Visitors can observe the pair of bald eagles nesting at Bombay Hook. Other birds of prey frequently spotted on the refuge are northern harriers and osprey.

Mammals Many of the mammals at Bombay Hook tend to mask their presence under darkness and by secrecy. The evidence of their coming and going is seen more than their actual presence, like the muskrat houses in the marshes. However, a keen eye and patience may provide a glimpse of an otter or beaver in a freshwater impoundment; you may stare down a red fox for a splendid moment at a field's edge before it trots lightly back into the woodlands.

Reptiles and amphibians Like mammals, reptiles and amphibians can be secretive. That does not mean they don't thrive at Bombay Hook. Northern water snakes, which can live in both freshwater and brackish water, are abundant. So are eastern garter snakes. Snapping turtles and diamondback terrapins sometimes lay their eggs in the soil of trails and even on the auto-tour road. Frogs are common in the freshwater, but most are heard, not seen—and heard mainly after the refuge closes, in the dusk and darkness. Green tree frogs, spring peepers, and bullfrogs are among them.

Fish During the warm months, a patient observer can see typical tidal marsh fish in the water along and under Boardwalk Trail. Look for schooling sheepshead minnows, killifish, and mummichogs, all evidence that seaside marshes produce the nourishment for larger food fish and sport fish.

Invertebrates During the summer, the invertebrate that is perhaps the most noticeable and the most unwelcome is the pesky greenhead fly. More welcome is the fiddler crab, which lives in the salt marsh and is observable from Boardwalk Trail at low tide. Small holes in the mud mark the openings of the burrows dug by these tiny crabs. It is easy to distinguish their sexes; males have one claw—the

THE HORSESHOE CRAB–SHOREBIRD CONNECTION Horseshoe crabs crawled out of the sea to breed long before small, primitive reptiles evolved into dinosaurs, and even longer before dinosaurs gave rise to birds. Somewhere along the line, shorebirds migrating north from wintering grounds in the southern Americas began to depend on the glutinous eggs of the female horseshoe crab for fuel on the last leg of their trip to the Arctic and its environs. Since the largest horseshoe crab population on earth inhabits Delaware Bay, at one point in time, probably after the last Ice Age, shorebirds began using it as do long-haul truckers at their first food stops. Eat all you can, take a break, then head out again.

Female horseshoe crabs lay their eggs just a bit too deeply in the sand for the long bills of shorebirds to reach them. But the more crabs that lay eggs, the more the eggs are roiled up—and the surf does its own roiling, too. So shorebirds can eat their fill.

Or, at least, have eaten their fill. Horseshoe-crab numbers have dwindled over the years. People use them for bait—a good way to catch real crabs, winkles, and eels. Regulations now control the harvest of horseshoe crabs to help the crab population sustain itself. However, some biologists wonder if diminishing numbers of crabs can sustain the shorebirds that depend on them for the fuel they need to reach their breeding grounds. It is a nature connection that needs inquiry.

fiddle—that is much larger than the other. The big claw is studded with minuscule bumps that the males use to duke it out during contests with other males over territory and the right to females. Fiddlers are food for many other creatures, ranging from birds to raccoons.

But the crab that is most important to the pyramid of life at Bombay Hook is not a crab at all. The horseshoe crab is actually a relative of spiders, but in a class by itself. It may not be a true crab, but it is a true blueblood. Its bluish blood, based on copper, has been used worldwide to test injectable drugs and medical equipment against germs harmful to humans.

Delaware Bay is home to the world's largest population of horseshoe crabs. From May through June—the last half of May is the peak—the crabs come ashore on sandy beaches just after the high tide peaks, where they perform a procreation ritual more than 350 million years old. The smaller males sluggishly jostle and struggle to mount females, which arrive on the beach shortly after they do. Key horseshoe crab beaches can have a mile or even miles of crabs in and above the wave wash, one atop the other, often in a swathe three or four yards wide. After external fertilization, females lay their eggs in the sand. For many crabs, the relentless urge to procreate ends in death. If a horseshoe crab is turned on its back by waves it cannot right itself. With unprotected underparts exposed, a horseshoe crab is easy prey for ravenous gulls. Concerned human beach walkers, at least those in the know, will often return overturned crabs to their proper position.

The best place to see the mass spawning of horseshoe crabs around Bombay Hook is at Pickering Beach, about a dozen miles south on Route 9. Turn left on Pickering Beach Road. Go a mile to its end, the site of a small beachfront community. Park where the signs—posted by the Pickering Beach Company—indicate. Access to the beach is through a path between two fences.

ACTIVITIES

■ **WILDLIFE OBSERVATION:** For waterbirds in the salt marsh, time your visit to the ebbing tide, when mudflats are exposed. At high tide, many birds tend to congregate in the freshwater impoundments, where water levels are manipulated by wildlife managers.

■ **PHOTOGRAPHY:** There are no special facilities for photographers. However, the auto tour and walking trails offer many opportunities.

■ **HIKES AND WALKS:** The official trails offer the best walking. There is no hardcore hiking here. Although it is not encouraged, you can park by the side of the auto tour and walk about. But the best walking is on the trails.

■ **SEASONAL EVENTS:** Each spring and fall, usually in May and October, the refuge offers all-day programs for the general public, including wildlife management tours, trail walks, wildlife talks, and boat and canoe trips. Contact the refuge for more details.

■ **PUBLICATIONS:** General refuge guide; pamphlets on the auto tour and trails; checklists of birds, fish, invertebrates, mammals, and amphibians and reptiles; and pamphlets (children and adult) on the shorebird–horseshoe crab connection.

HUNTING AND FISHING
Both **deer** and **waterfowl** seasons open in the fall, in accordance with the state seasons. Deer hunts are granted by a preseason drawing; waterfowl hunts are granted through a daily drawing.

There is no fishing on the refuge.

Prime Hook NWR
Milton, Delaware

Tidal-freshwater marsh, Prime Hook NWR

Many residents of the First State knew from the outset that Prime Hook NWR, established in 1963, was a treasure. Delaware birders and waterfowl hunters flocked here, drawn by great hosts of migratory waterfowl that arrive each spring and fall.

Ironically, although Prime Hook lies on the shores of Delaware Bay, it is currently shut off from the sea by a thin strip of development, mostly beach communities. Nevertheless, it has marshes where tidal water and freshwater mingle and, as its crowning glory, a 2,500-acre freshwater impoundment that is one of the largest of its kind on the East Coast. Although intensely managed, this vast wetland has the aspect of a true watery wilderness, with wandering creeks, woody swamps, and marshes that seem to reach the horizon. Wetlands are Prime Hook's main draw for waterfowl and a host of other aquatic birds—and the visitors who come to enjoy them. The refuge's scattered woodlands, where songbirds rest during migration and where a goodly number of them nest, are an added perk.

The public beyond Delaware's borders has begun to discover Prime Hook, which now boasts a homey headquarters building enclosing a small but handsome Visitor Center. In back of the building is a charming garden for butterflies and hummingbirds, complete with a gurgling waterfall.

HISTORY

Covering almost 9,000 acres, Prime Hook was established primarily to preserve coastal wetlands as habitat in which migratory waterfowl could winter and breed. Many of the public facilities at the refuge are the work of volunteers, a loyal cadre composed mostly of hunters who erect osprey platforms and deer stands and who, when funding ran out for construction of the headquarters building, which opened in 1997, finished the structure, gratis.

The Visitor Center sports a glassed-in mural, depicting Canada geese and black ducks—one of which has a band on its leg—flying over the Prime Hook marshes. Wildlife artist Richard Clifton, whose work has graced myriad state duck stamps, is the muralist. He is a Delaware local, and Prime Hook is where he goes to paint his waterfowl.

GETTING THERE

Prime Hook headquarters is 12 mi. southeast of Milford and 10 mi. north of Lewes. From Rte. 1, take Rte. 16 east for 1 mi. Turn left and go 1.6 mi. to the office.

■ **SEASON:** Refuge open year-round.

■ **HOURS:** Refuge open: sunrise to sunset. Headquarters, including the Visitor Center, open 7:30 a.m.-4 p.m. weekdays. Visitor Center is staffed by volunteers from 9 a.m.–4 p.m., Sat., Sun., and holidays, April 1–Nov. 1.

■ **FEES:** None for refuge entry. Duck blinds, first-come, first-serve in season, $5 per hunter. Boat launch to the main impoundment (behind headquarters), $1. Deer hunting, $5.

■ **ADDRESS:** Prime Hook NWR, RD 3, Box 195, Milton, DE 19968

■ **TELEPHONE:** 302/684-8419

TOURING PRIME HOOK

■ **BY AUTOMOBILE:** The refuge has no formal auto tour; public roads cross the refuge, however. Rte. 16, east of the refuge entrance, bisects a brackish marsh on the south and the major freshwater impoundment on the north. A great variety of waterbirds can be seen in season. To the north, Prime Hook Beach Rd. also bisects marshes that host aquatic birds. Osprey platforms are located by roadside. It's best not to leave your vehicle to observe nesting ospreys so as not to disturb them. North of that, shorebirds can also be seen along Fowler Beach Rd.

■ **BY FOOT:** Prime Hook offers four short walking trails through various habitats, with many good views over impoundments. The entrance road also affords good walking.

■ **BY BICYCLE:** The refuge has no trails specifically for biking, but public roads through the refuge are suitable.

Gadwall ducks

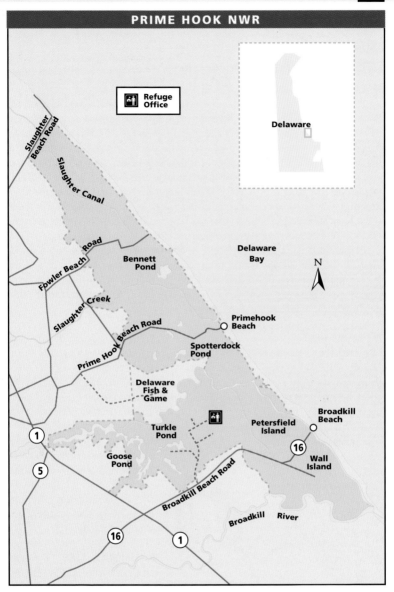

PRIME HOOK NWR

Refuge Office

Delaware

Slaughter Beach Road

Slaughter Canal

Fowler Beach Road

Bennett Pond

Delaware Bay

N

Slaughter Creek

Prime Hook Beach Road

Primehook Beach

Spotterdock Pond

Delaware Fish & Game

Turkle Pond

Petersfield Island

Broadkill Beach

1

Goose Pond

Broadkill Beach Road

Wall Island

16

5

16

1

Broadkill River

■ **BY CANOE, KAYAK, OR BOAT:** Canoeing and small boating (25 hp or less) are great ways to get hooked on Prime Hook: The refuge has more than 15 miles of waterways to explore, all gentle going. A boat launch behind headquarters provides entry into the major impoundment. It is used mostly by waterfowlers but is a quick way for anyone to gain marsh access. Powered boats inside the refuge are restricted to motors of 25 hp or less. A canoe trail winds for 7 miles along Prime Hook Creek, starting north of headquarters off Route 1 and ending at headquarters, in the major impoundment (a pamphlet for a self-guided canoe tour is available at the Visitor Center). There is a privately owned parking area on the east of Route 1 by Waples Pond, but a portage through thick brush is required to reach the creek. Easier: Park for a small fee at a commercial family park just south of the state area, pay a small fee ($7), and launch. The entire trail is open March 15 to October 15. Only the westernmost 4 miles are open for the rest of the year, with access from Waples Pond only.

WHAT TO SEE

■ **LANDSCAPE AND CLIMATE** Prime Hook, like Bombay Hook to the north, is a fertile lowland by the sea. Just behind the sandy beaches of Delaware Bay lie estuaries, fed by small rivers and creeks. Within these marshes, a war goes on, as it had since the beginning of the last Ice Age, when the level of the sea rose to cover the eastern fringe of North America. The conflict is between the inward march of saline waters against the outward flow of the fresh. Under natural conditions, an ecological armistice of sorts would be achieved, with habitats changing according to the order of nature, providing for give-and-take that over time engenders a healthful balance. Given changes in habitat caused by humans, the water levels in 4,200 acres of marshes at Prime Hook must be manipulated, raised and lowered at different times of year to create optimum conditions for plants and animals.

Prime Hook has a relatively moderate climate, given its position on the middle Atlantic coast. During winter, however, storms may roar in from the sea, and June to September can be hot and sultry. During the summer, biting insects prosper. As annoying as they may be to visitors, they are an important food resource for shorebirds and breeding wood ducks.

■ **PLANT LIFE**

Freshwater marshes Canoe Trail is perhaps the best way to view Prime Hook's most interesting wetlands plants. Vegetation by the side of the creek includes red maples, sweetbay magnolia, increasingly rare Atlantic white cedar, winterberry, and bayberry. Pickerelweed, arrowhead, and water lilies lie in more open water. A key reason for managing water levels in the freshwater marshes is to encourage the growth of wild millet and rice, major foods for waterfowl.

Red maple leaf and seedpod

Uplands The upland woodlands of Prime Hook are typical of southern Delaware forests, with a mix of oaks, hickories, and other deciduous trees and pines typical of the south, such as Virginia and loblolly.

■ **ANIMAL LIFE** Like other refuges on the middle Atlantic coast, Prime Hook is known for its birds. This is waterbird and, to a lesser extent, migrant-songbird territory. Even though many mammals inhabit the refuge, they are seldom seen or heard, with a few exceptions. You may be able to observe several types of reptiles and amphibians.

Birds The legions of migratory waterfowl visiting Prime Hook are like the special effects in a blockbuster sci-fi movie. They overwhelm the senses. In the fall, they arrive en masse: some 50,000 ducks, including black ducks, gadwalls, pintails, shovelers, teal, and more than 100,000 snow geese. Black-necked stilts, evocative of long-legged adolescents in tuxedoes, also nest there (about 40 pair). These are not uncommon birds, but they are rarely seen.

Among the ducks are many that are at home on the fringes of the sea and inland waters—gadwalls and black ducks, for example. Because of its vast fresh-water marshes, Prime Hook also hosts a significant population of wood ducks, which many people consider the most beautiful duck in North America. This bird prefers wetland habitats with trees. You will have a good chance of seeing the wood duck at Prime Hook around the freshwater impoundment.

The warm sun of May brings myriad warblers. These feathered jewels are so abundant that droves of them can be seen picking up grit and foraging on the road that leads in and out of refuge headquarters.

During the spring and fall, shorebirds pass through the refuge. Searching for ospreys? Prime Hook has several breeding pairs. It is not unusual for visitors to see them catching fish.

Endangered Delmarva fox squirrel

Mammals Especially in early morning and before dusk, you have a good chance of spotting white-tailed deer. Prime Hook is also home to otters, raccoons, red foxes, and muskrats. Of them all, muskrats are the easiest to find because they are most active during the day, in freshwater and brackish marshes. If muskrats are not visible, their homes certainly are: domes of reeds and other aquatic vegetation standing in shallow water. And muskrat droppings are often seen on rocks and logs just above water level.

Prime Hook is a refuge for the endangered Delmarva fox squirrel. This species is seldom seen, but signs along the entrance road warn drivers to give way to them if they should cross.

Reptiles and amphibians Like mammals, reptiles and amphibians are secretive, often nocturnal. Canoeists, though, have an excellent chance to see painted turtles, bullfrogs, and northern water snakes.

ACTIVITIES

■ **CAMPING:** Camping is not allowed on the refuge, but campsites (some oceanfront) are available at Cape Henlopen State Park, 15 miles north of the refuge, in Lewes (302/645-8983).

■ **WILDLIFE OBSERVATION:** Spring and fall are the best birding times, but, if you have warm clothing and want to see waterfowl, winter is not bad. Check with Visitor Center about areas closed to the general public during hunting season.

■ **PHOTOGRAPHY:** The duck blinds may be helpful for photographers with telephoto lenses. There are no observation towers. However, there are many pull-offs on public roads that offer good photo access. If you are not worried about your photo equipment getting wet, Canoe Trail can get your lens close up with nature—if you are lucky.

■ **HIKES AND WALKS:** Board-walk Trail through the freshwater impoundment behind headquarters is 0.5 mile. Black Farm Trail through managed croplands and woodlands is a 1.2-mile round-trip. Pine Grove Trail near Fleetwood and Turkle (the local term for *turtle*) ponds is an eighth of a mile loop. Dike Trail is 1.0 mile round-trip.

■ **SEASONAL EVENTS:** Bird Festival in summer.

■ **PUBLICATIONS:** Bird list; refuge brochure.

HUNTING AND FISHING: It is no accident that hunters are among the main volunteers helping Prime Hook. In its freshwater marsh, 3,000 **waterfowl** are harvested each fall. The refuge also draws large numbers of **white-tailed deer** hunters. It has 160 deer stands, built by volunteers. The marsh also produces lunker **large-mouth bass** and **panfish**.

Blackwater NWR
Dorchester County, Maryland

Sunset, Blackwater NWR

Vast brackish marshes, freshwater impoundments, and seasonally flooded forest dominated by loblolly pines—a woodland reminiscent of times before logging and farming changed the landscape of the Eastern Shore of Chesapeake Bay. This is Blackwater NWR, where tundra swans winter after a transcontinental journey from their breeding grounds on the treeless shores of the Arctic Ocean; where American bald eagles nest in the greatest densities north of Florida (in the lower 48 states, that is). Sleek Atlantic Flyway Canada geese, more wild and far fewer in number than the bulky resident honkers, stay a while, after the cold drives them from northeastern Canada. Here, too, the Delmarva fox squirrel, endangered, scurries beneath the pines in search of seeds and acorns. Indeed, Blackwater has wildlife in overwhelming abundance. But it has another claim to fame: Dominating the marshes is a sedge, half as tall as a man, known as the Olney three-square bulrush. Its triangular stem is topped by a seed cluster. The Blackwater area is the northernmost margin of the Olney bulrush's range.

HISTORY

Before the arrival of European settlers, a group of Native Americans known as the Nanticoke split off from the Delaware tribe, to the east, and established themselves in the Blackwater area. Early in the 16th century, settlers from Europe began to enter the region; Captain John Smith was one of the first to visit. Settlement spelled the end for most of the continuous forest and many wetlands. Traces of old agricultural furrows and drainage ditches can still be detected on its damp floor. Even so, the loblolly forest has regrown, and brackish marshes not readily convertible to farmland remain largely intact. The marsh also survived because of its wealth of resources; it attracted waterfowl and muskrats, used for food and trapping, respectively. Most of the refuge's marshes, in fact, were formerly fur farms where muskrats were harvested. The marshes, with their benefits

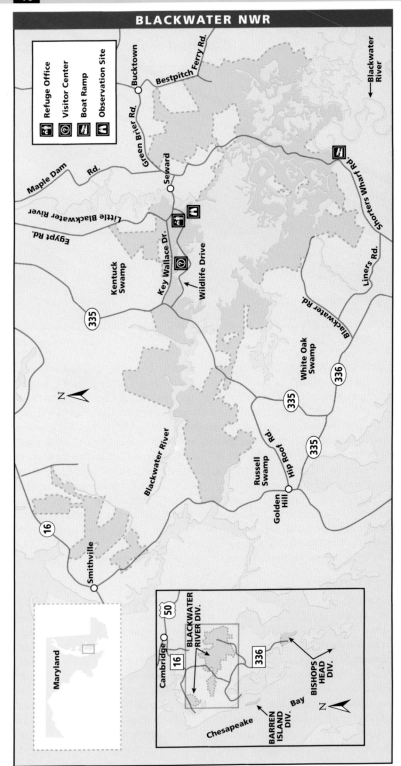

BLACKWATER NWR

for waterfowl, were the reason for establishing Blackwater NWR in 1933. The refuge was originally 8,600 acres and has since grown to 24,000 acres. The heart of the refuge, and the area designated for public use, lies about 10 miles inland from Chesapeake Bay. However, outlying portions of Blackwater extend to the bay itself.

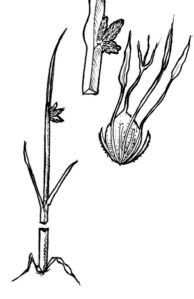

Olney three-square bulrush

GETTING THERE

Blackwater is 12 mi. south of Cambridge. From Rte. 50, take Rte. 16 South. Go 7 mi. to Church Creek, turn left on to Rte. 335 South, then left on Key Wallace Dr. and follow signs to the refuge.

■ **SEASON:** The refuge is open year-round.

■ **HOURS:** General refuge: sunrise to sunset. Visitor Center: 8 a.m.–4 p.m. weekdays; 9 a.m–5 p.m., weekends; closed Christmas and Thanksgiving. Headquarters: 8 a.m.–4:30 p.m., weekdays.

■ **FEES:** Entrance fee $3 per vehicle, $1 per pedestrian or bicyclist.

■ **ADDRESS:** Blackwater NWR, 2145 Key Wallace Dr., Cambridge, MD 21613

■ **TELEPHONE:** 410/228-2692

TOURING BLACKWATER

■ **BY AUTOMOBILE:** Most visitors tour the refuge in vehicles, along a paved, 3.5-mile wildlife drive that affords views of both marshes and forest. Freshwater marsh is on one side of the drive, brackish on the other, as it passes through good samples of the refuge's main habitats: tidal marsh, freshwater ponds and impoundments, and forest.

■ **BY FOOT:** Walkers are permitted on the wildlife drive. Two walking paths, Woods Trail (0.5 mile) and Marsh Edge Trail (0.3 mile), lead off the drive.

■ **BY BICYCLE:** Bikers may use the wildlife drive but not the trails.

■ **BY BOAT, CANOE, OR KAYAK:** Boating is permitted, generally from April 1 to Sept. 31. There are no boat launches on the refuge, but there is a launch at Shorter's Wharf on Shorter's Wharf Rd., east of the Visitor Center.

WHAT TO SEE

■ **LANDSCAPE AND CLIMATE** The best times to visit Blackwater, weather-wise, as well as for wildlife viewing, are spring and fall. Spring arrives early; fall stays late. In between those seasons, summers can be hot, winters are usually damp, with occasional severe weather, but cold snaps and snows of any measure are transient.

Situated on the Atlantic Coastal Plain, Blackwater is flat and much of it barely above sea level. The level of the sea, for that matter, is encroaching upon the refuge at a rate of a half-foot a century, about twice that of the rest of the Middle Atlantic shore (see Regional Overview). The rise is a result not only of the sea's advance

OUR NATIONAL SYMBOL The American bald eagle, with its white head (when mature), yellow hooked beak, and broad wings, has a regal appearance. But looks are sometimes deceiving. Benjamin Franklin thought that the wild turkey—wild and wary in his days—would be a better symbol of the nation than the bald eagle. Franklin had a point.

The bald eagle is a mugger, a thief, and a scavenger and likes to eat leftovers. No doubt, our avian king is an aggressive predator. A merganser or a migrating salmon, hooked in the water by the eagle's terrifying talons, is truly dead meat. In fact, the bald eagle may even prefer dead meat, creatures that have already expired. It haunts waters where things die. In Alaska, the brown bears fish the salmon; eagles take the remains. Mergansers are fish-eating ducks. Bald eagles watch them from perches or while soaring overhead. If a merganser surfaces with a fish, the eagle may swoop down upon it, grabbing the fish—and maybe the merganser.

The bald eagle's main target is the osprey. The two species often engage in aerial combat over the marshes of Blackwater. The osprey, long-winged but slight of build compared with the eagle, soars and hovers, then plunges, sometimes from hundreds of feet, from air to water, rocketing back into the air with a fish in its talons. Enter the eagle. It harasses the osprey, buzzing it like a fighter plane going after a B-52 bomber, except that sizes are reversed. Frustrated, the osprey will often drop its fish, down into the water, whereupon the eagle dives and retrieves it. Corporate raiders have nothing on this robber bird.

but also the sinking of the land. Marshes, as a result, are being drowned. New marshes form upriver, but they can only go so far. Outside the refuge, the landscape has been so changed by agriculture and other development that marshes can no longer evolve.

■ **PLANT LIFE** Most people come to Blackwater to watch animals. But to understand the animals, we need to look at the plant communities that support them. The loblolly pine and the three-square bulrush each dominates its own community, and each provides certain essentials for some of the refuge's most important creatures.

Marshlands The Olney three-square bulrush is primarily a freshwater plant but also does quite well in the brackish waters of Blackwater. The give-and-take of sea tides, coastal storms, and freshwater runoff varies the salinity of the marshes. The water never becomes highly saline, which allows the bulrush to flourish. The bulrush is a boon for the number-one mammal of the marshes, the muskrat, furnishing food and building material for the dome-shaped lodges in which this rodent lives. (Muskrats also live in bank burrows.)

Cattails, unlike bulrushes, are primarily confined to fresh waters of the refuge. Close to the margins of the Chesapeake, cordgrasses make their appearance. Their niche is determined by moderate to high salinity. The bulrush cannot tolerate salt the way cordgrass does. Cordgrass, on the other hand, dwindles as water freshens.

Forests Although Blackwater brings marshes to mind, almost half of the refuge is covered in forest, dominated by loblolly pine. Scattered about are oaks, chiefly white and red, as well a few hickories. The forest floor is shaded and, also because of seasonal flooding, open—the perfect habitat for the Delmarva fox squirrel to

Bald eagle

forage, since it likes searching for food on the ground more than in the trees, as do gray squirrels. And the forest floor has food in good supply: pine seeds, acorns, and the occasional hickory nut that squirrels, whether fox or gray, dearly love.

During the spring, the understory of the Coastal Plain pine forest comes alive with white flowers of dogwood. Alert: Poison ivy spreads here and there as does its "leaves of three" look-alike, the Virginia creeper. Ground pine carpets much of the floor, and mayapples bloom there.

■ **ANIMAL LIFE** Even a casual observer can see a fine variety of animals at Blackwater. All you have to do is look up in the air, look across the marshes, or even look down at the ground.

Birds Blackwater was founded to protect ducks, but its main attraction today is probably the bald eagle, which has been known to eat a duck or two. More than a dozen pair of these great birds nest there. On the average, each eagle nest fledges two young. During summer, plenty of eagles may be seen; during the winter, there are even more. Up to 150 eagles winter at Blackwater on a regular basis.

The refuge also has a history of protecting ospreys. In the 1960s, ospreys, along with eagles and peregrine falcons, were vanishing from much of their original range due to the negative impact of pesticides on their reproductive systems. Significant numbers of ospreys, however, remained in the Chesapeake Bay area. Conservationists took eggs from nests in the Chesapeake and used the young that were produced to restock places where these "fish hawks" had become rare. Many of the ospreys that now teem in southern New England, for example, are of Chesapeake lineage.

Ducks congregate by the thousands at Blackwater, especially in the spring and fall. Mallards, blue-winged teal, green-winged teal, wigeon, and pintails arrive on their migration. Some leave, some stay and nest or winter over. During the winter, the refuge offers a chance to see several hundred tundra swans, regal birds, their black bills notched with yellow, that winter only in the middle Atlantic and a few places west of the Rockies. Seeing them here, for a birder who can't get out to their western nesting grounds, is a rare treat.

Fall brings the Atlantic Flyway geese to the refuge. Their graceful V formations head for the refuge unerringly. Sighting the marshes, the geese spread their wings and break their flight. They settle gracefully on open water to feed and rest.

Mammals A sharp eye can sometimes discern muskrats in the marshes. The

Nutria

ridge of their back and their eyes, ears, and nose are visible above the water. With oarlike tails, muskrats scull to and fro. Another water-loving rodent lives here, too. It resembles the muskrat superficially but is half again as large and has a round tail. This is the nutria, a South American creature introduced here years ago, so it could be trapped for its fur. Like many introductions of exotic species, the transference of the nutria has proven to be a bad move. Nutria devour bulrushes, a precious food source, always struggling to sustain itself in the brackish marshlands. Refuge managers have mounted a program to control this rodent. Still, for good or ill, it is an interesting sight for a visitor.

Another introduced mammal is the sika deer, from Asia. A relative of the American elk, or wapiti, the sika is smaller than the native white-tailed deer with which it shares the refuge. The natural habitat of the sika deer ranges from eastern Siberia and Manchuria to Japan, and south to Vietnam and Taiwan. Most native populations of sika deer are imperiled. Ironically, those that have been introduced outside their original range—in places such as Europe and New Zealand as well as Maryland and Virginia—seem to be faring far better than their relatives back home. Blackwater is an ideal spot for this species of deer because, although it likes forest, it adapts well to swamps and marshes.

Both the white-tailed deer and sika can be seen at Blackwater. Because it is often active by day, the white-tailed deer is easier to find, while the sika is primarily nocturnal. It's easy to distinguish adult sikas from adult whitetails. As fawns, both are spotted with white. Whitetails lose the spots within a few months. Sika deer, as a rule, retain them through adult life.

ACTIVITIES

■ **CAMPING:** No camping is allowed on the refuge, but camping facilities are available at Taylor's Island Campground, 20 miles from the refuge.

■ **WILDLIFE OBSERVATION:** Wildlife-viewing opportunities are excellent year-round at Blackwater. Even in midwinter, there is much to see. Resident bald eagles are rebuilding their nests in the pines, and the wintering group has arrived.

The pines on these mounds of dry land rising from the marsh are prime bald eagle nesting sites. Bald eagles are especially sensitive to disturbance when courting, incubating their eggs, or rearing their young. Surrounded by wetlands, the hummocks provide the isolation that parent eagles require to rear a family successfully.

Remarkably, wintering golden eagles, usually a species of remote wilderness, can sometimes be seen from the wildlife drive. Many Canada geese and ducks remain at the refuge throughout the winter.

Early spring brings more ducks to the refuge, although not as many as in fall, and they tend to pass through quickly. May is a good time to see warblers and white-tailed fawns. By August, eaglets have fledged and young ospreys are leaving their nests—staying on, however, for at least a month before they migrate south. The numbers of egrets and herons mount as northern migrants join the birds that have been on the refuge since spring. And the shorebirds, weeks away from their northern birding grounds, are winging in to feed and rest before retreating south of the border.

■ **PHOTOGRAPHY:** Because the wildlife drive is atop a dike, it affords an overview of marshes, and birds are often seen from here, close by. Both walking trails also draw photographers.

■ **HIKES AND WALKS:** Marsh Edge Trail provides a mini tour of key Blackwater habitats. It starts in pine forest, where you may be able to see Delmarva fox squirrels on the ground, and ends on a boardwalk through bulrushes and cattails, offering views of waterbirds, including several species of ducks.

Woods Trail traverses mature pine forest. Here again, fox squirrels scurry over the ground. In season, this is a good spot to see and hear warblers.

These trails are extremely easy going. The Blackwater outdoor experience is not meant to be a physical challenge but to bring people close up with nature as easily as possible.

> **HUNTING AND FISHING** Deer hunting—both **white-tailed** and **sika**—is permitted from Oct. through Dec. There are youth and muzzle-loader hunts, both of which require special permits. Contact the refuge for details. The fishing season runs from April through Sept. Species most often found include **catfish**, **largemouth bass**, and **white** and **yellow perch**.

■ **SEASONAL EVENTS:** May: Spring Fling, first weekend of the month; October: Open House, third weekend of the month, during National Wildlife Refuge Week. Both events have a country-fair atmosphere with entertainment, demonstrations of bird banding, and presentations by biologists. Tours into areas of the refuge that usually are off limits are offered.

■ **PUBLICATIONS:** Blackwater Visitor Center has a full-fledged bookstore and gift shop, plus a library of videotapes on topics relating to the refuge and on environmental conservation in general. On request, visitors may view the videos at the center. The refuge publishes a variety of natural history pamphlets.

Eastern Neck NWR
Rock Hall, Maryland

Spartina grass, salt marsh

It has been called one of the national wildlife refuge system's best-kept secrets. Indeed, Eastern Neck NWR qualifies as a secret place, despite its location within sight of the Chesapeake Bay Bridge and, as the crow flies, some 15 miles from Annapolis. But that doesn't make this island in the mouth of the Chester River easy to access. To get to Eastern Neck from where the bridge meets the Eastern Shore requires a round-trip of some 50 miles on corkscrew roads that wind around multiple inlets and creeks of the estuaries.

For the tundra swan, which nests in the Arctic, and thousands of other migrating waterfowl, however, Eastern Neck is no secret. In fall and winter the waters and marshes surrounding the island are full of waterfowl, which rest here to avoid the northern chill. For human visitors, the level landscape of the island and its location in the bay allow magnificent sunrise and sunset views, enhanced by the sight of thousands of birds rising from the water to greet the day.

HISTORY

The Ozinies, a small group of Algonquinian speakers, were the predominant Native Americans when Captain John Smith visited the area in the early 1600s. Shell middens on the beach show that the Indians camped and harvested shellfish here. Flat and fertile, the island was farmed for generations, becoming a base for Chesapeake watermen, who earned a living oystering and crabbing. This idyllic life was threatened in the 1950s. A real estate developer purchased land on the island with the idea of subdividing it into 293 home lots. The subdivision was a bust: Only one house was built. In 1962, the U.S. Fish & Wildlife Service purchased the land, and the refuge spread eventually over 2,285 acres, a haven in the mouth of the Chester River. The one house built by the developer did not languish, however: It is currently in use as the refuge headquarters while the new Visitor Center, in a beautiful old hunting lodge on the property, is being readied for use.

GETTING THERE

Eastern Neck is 20 mi. south of Chestertown, Maryland. But from any direction, it takes time just to get to Chestertown. From the north, take MD 213 to Chestertown. From the south, and the bay bridge, go north on US 301, then north on MD 213 to Chestertown. MD 20 goes west from Chestertown to Rock Hall. From there, turn south on CR 445 to the refuge. A charming wooden bridge over Eastern Neck Narrows links the refuge to the mainland.

■ **SEASON:** General refuge open year-round, sunrise to a half-hour before sunset.

■ **HOURS:** Headquarters open 7 a.m.–4 p.m., weekdays. Headquarters does not yet have a Visitor Center, per se, but does offer a small bookstore.

■ **ADDRESS:** Eastern Neck NWR, 1730 Eastern Neck Rd., Rock Hall, MD 21662

■ **TELEPHONE:** 410/639-7056

TOURING EASTERN NECK

■ **BY AUTOMOBILE:** There is no designated auto-tour route at Eastern Neck, but several county roads run through the refuge, with Eastern Neck Rd. slicing down its center, north and south. The road passes through typical refuge habitats, including pine forest and marshes.

■ **BY FOOT:** The refuge has four designated trails and a boardwalk at Tubby Cove.

■ **BY BICYCLE:** Bikers may use the refuge's three miles of county roads as well as the gravelled refuge roads open to public vehicles.

■ **BY BOAT, CANOE, OR KAYAK:** Boating is a good way to explore the margins of the refuge. Car-top watercraft may be launched at Ingleside and at Bogles Wharf Landing. The landing also has a boat ramp, but requires a county permit.

Bufflehead

WHAT TO SEE

■ **LANDSCAPE AND CLIMATE** The climate at Eastern Neck is relatively warm, year-round; you're at the same latitude, approximately, as Washington, DC. Being surrounded by water further moderates the weather; but remember, summer weather on Chesapeake Bay can sometimes be uncomfortable.

The sandy soils underlying the refuge are visible on the bluffs, eroded steadily for many years due to currents coursing down the Chester River and through the bay. Breakwaters, consisting of large stones, were built to protect the bluffs. Sand dredged up from Kent Narrows, southwest of the refuge, was used to create several acres of marshland at the end of the breakwaters. Volunteers planted thousands of cordgrass plants to anchor the dredged material, and a new tidal marsh was created for waterfowl.

Managers at the refuge have also set up five freshwater impoundments, called greentree reservoirs, where woodlands are flooded during winter, when

EASTERN NECK NWR

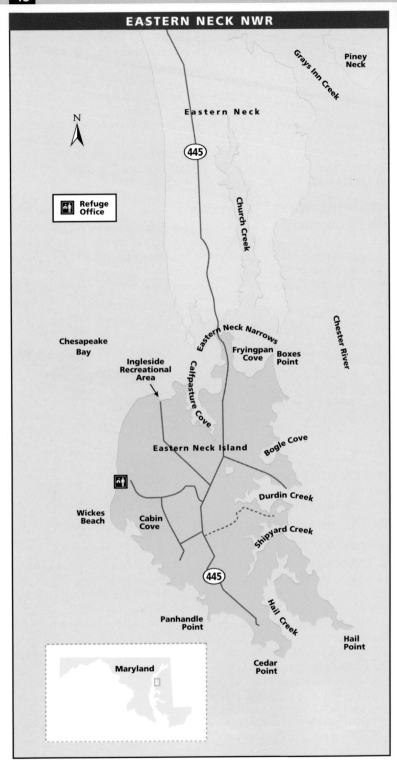

Piney Neck

Grays Inn Creek

Eastern Neck

N

445

Refuge Office

Church Creek

Chester River

Chesapeake Bay

Eastern Neck Narrows

Fryingpan Cove

Boxes Point

Ingleside Recreational Area

Calfpasture Cove

Eastern Neck Island

Bogle Cove

Durdin Creek

Wickes Beach

Cabin Cove

Shipyard Creek

445

Panhandle Point

Hail Creek

Hail Point

Cedar Point

Maryland

trees are dormant. This process creates wintering habitat for waterfowl and encourages the growth of small invertebrates in the leaf litter.

■ **PLANT LIFE** For such a small place, Eastern Neck has a remarkable variety of plant communities. Some are the result of human management, while others are natural. In a sense the refuge is a microcosm of the plant life existing in the entire mid-Atlantic coastal region.

Tidal marshes About 1,000 acres of brackish marsh rim the refuge. Here grow the cordgrasses—salt marsh cordgrass in low-lying areas and salt meadow cordgrass on slightly higher ground that is only occasionally flooded by the tides. Still farther upland are bulrushes and needlerush, which can withstand only low levels of salinity.

Woodlands Loblolly pines, with scattered chestnut oaks and hickories and a thick understory of holly and pawpaw, are in the majority in the Eastern Neck forests, covering about 500 acres of the refuge. Other woodlands consist mostly of hardwoods, such as popular, sweet gum and oak species.

Agricultural fields The island was farmed for generations by year-round residents. About 500 acres are still under cultivation by a farmer from outside the refuge, who plants wildlife food plots as payment for the right to use cropland. The farmer harvests corn, soybeans, and wheat; some of the grain is usually left unharvested, solely to feed waterfowl and other birds. When the crop is standing, songbirds find cover there.

■ **ANIMAL LIFE** As at other refuges on the Atlantic Coastal Plain, birds are Eastern Neck's big attraction. But there are some mammalian and insect surprises in store for visitors, too.

Birds Almost 250 species of birds have been seen at Eastern Neck. The most spectacular of these, arguably, is the tundra swan, once known as the whistling swan because of its haunting call, a sound reminiscent of the Arctic barrens on which this regal bird breeds.

Waterfowl come to this refuge during fall and winter—by the thousands. They

Tundra (whistling) swans

are plentiful here, although not in the truly immense numbers that visit other Middle Atlantic refuges. It is the variety of waterfowl species that makes Eastern Neck a treat. This refuge draws ducks of shallows, bay, and sea, 30 species of waterfowl in all. Bay ducks include redheads, ruddy ducks, scaups, ring-necks, and canvasbacks. Dabbling ducks, which skim shallows for food, include mallards, black ducks, wigeon, and northern pintail. From the sea come buffleheads and white-winged scoters (flashing feathers of black and white) and old-squaws (the males of the species boast a pennant of tail feathers).

Eastern Neck has additional rewards for enthusiastic birders who make the 50-mile round-trip to the island: Bald eagles and osprey nest here, and from spring through fall you will find a host of wading birds as well.

Mammals White-tailed deer love Eastern Neck. Your chances of seeing them by the roadside are good. Woodchucks can also be seen at the curb of the road, nibbling on vegetation. (Better there than in your garden.) If there is a mammal that is a star at Eastern Neck, however, it is the red fox. Secretive and usually nocturnal, these resilient and graceful animals abound here and can sometimes be seen near roads in the fading or rising light of the sun.

Invertebrates Wildlife managers at Eastern Neck built their butterfly trail for

Tubby Cove boardwalk, Eastern Neck NWR

a very good reason. More than two dozen species of butterflies have been observed on the refuge. Look especially for the zebra swallowtail, a species dependent upon the presence of pawpaw in the forest understory.

ACTIVITIES

■ **WILDLIFE OBSERVATION:** Many types of wildlife can be seen from Eastern Neck Road, as well as other roads within the refuge. From Eastern Neck refuge, it's easy to reach Kent County Ingleside Recreation Area, where visitors can picnic and go crabbing. Wildlife trails lead off the roads. A plus: In summer you can pick blackberries and raspberries along the roadsides.

On the refuge, head to the wooden bridge to see tundra swans and hawks winging over on fall migrations. The bridge and Tubby Cove boardwalk area is the best bet for spotting ducks in winter. You may spy the endangered Delmarva fox squirrel by following trails through the forest. Don't look up into the trees; scan the ground instead—that's where these squirrels forage. Eastern Neck is a haven for this species. Fox squirrels from Eastern Neck have been transplanted to other mid-Atlantic refuges, in order to restore their dwindling numbers and distribution.

■ **PHOTOGRAPHY:** The observation tower at Tubby Cove includes a blind, where the marshes and their many birds can be quietly photographed. The wooden bridge is another favorite site for photographers because of the numbers of waterfowl that gather there.

■ **HIKES AND WALKS:** The boardwalk at Tubby Cove enters marshland and provides access to the observation tower. Boxes Point Trail is 1.2 miles round-trip, and Duck Inn Trail is 1 mile, Wildlife Trail is a half-mile loop. The newest trail walkway is Bay View/Butterfly Trail, built by volunteers, leading from headquarters to an observation platform overlooking bluffs 25 feet high on the western shore of the island, with a magnificent view of the breakwaters project.

If you want a shaded woodland walk, take Wildlife Trail, in the center of the refuge. The other trails also pass through woods, but then lead out to the Chester River.

HUNTING AND FISHING Hunting season for **white-tailed deer** occurs in Sept. and Oct., by permit only. **Blue crabbing** is permitted and is best around July and Aug. Sport fish in the refuge waters include **striped bass** and **yellow perch**.

■ **PUBLICATIONS:** Refuge general leaflet with map, bird list, and other brochures. The refuge bookstore carries a variety of wildlife guidebooks and environmental education related products.

Patuxent Research Refuge
Laurel, Maryland

White-tailed deer foraging and bird blinds, Patuxent Research Refuge

Halfway between Baltimore, Maryland, and Washington, D.C., running alongside the bustling parkway linking the two cities, is a national wildlife refuge that is a microcosm of mid-Atlantic nature. It's a place where bald eagles nest and beavers create wetlands with their dams. Waterfowl are drawn by the thousands to its tranquil ponds, streams, and impoundments, and one of the largest forested areas in the mid-Atlantic provides critical nesting habitat for neotropical migratory birds. Patuxent is that rare place where visitors can immerse themselves in the wild without having to rough it.

Patuxent Research Refuge is the only national wildlife refuge established to support wildlife research, thus its special designation. Patuxent's three units include Central Tract, site of Patuxent Wildlife Research Center laboratories and facilities for breeding imperiled species, as well as field research areas; this unit is off-limits to visitors. But there is plenty of land to explore in North Tract, and in South Tract you will find one of the largest science and environmental education centers run by the Department of the Interior, with state-of-the-art exhibits (comparable to those in Washington's Smithsonian Institution) bringing you face-to-face with scientists' wildlife preservation techniques. The center's immediate environs are open to the public.

HISTORY

Patuxent is an Algonquin word for "when the water falls," referring to the little stair-step waterfalls that once were common on the Patuxent and Little Patuxent rivers. The refuge land, which lies on both sides of the rivers, owes its birth to an executive order by President Franklin Roosevelt in 1936, creating a refuge with the mission of conserving and protecting the nation's wildlife through both research and management techniques. Originally 2,670 acres, it is now 12,750 acres in size, largely due to the acquisition of land formerly managed by the U.S.

departments of Agriculture and Defense. For most of its existence, the entire refuge was closed to the public. The North Tract was opened in 1991.

GETTING THERE

The two visitable tracts at Patuxent are reached from the Baltimore-Washington Parkway but via different routes. To reach the Visitor Contact Station at North Tract (an access pass must be obtained there), go east for 1.4 mi. on MD 198 to the refuge entrance drive, south side of the road. To reach South Tract and the National Wildlife Visitor Center, take Powder Mill Rd. east for 2 mi. Once inside the refuge, follow signs to the Visitor Center.

■ **SEASON:** North Tract Visitor Contact Station is open daily year-round except for Thanksgiving, Christmas, and New Year's Day. South Tract Visitor Center is open daily year-round except for Christmas.

■ **HOURS:** North Tract and Visitor Contact Station: Nov.–Feb., 8 a.m.–4:30 p.m.; March, 8 a.m.–6 p.m.; April–Aug., 8 a.m.–8 p.m.; Sept., 8 a.m.–7 p.m.; Oct., 8 a.m.–6:30 p.m. South Tract National Wildlife Visitor Center: 10 a.m.–5:30 p.m., year-round. Patuxent refuge headquarters open 8 a.m.–4:30 p.m., weekends only, year-round.

■ **FEES:** None for refuge or Visitor Center. Tram tour: $2 adults, $1 children and seniors.

■ **ADDRESS:** Patuxent Research Refuge, 10901 Scarlet Tanager Loop, Laurel, MD 20708-4027

■ **TELEPHONE:** Headquarters: 301/497-5580; Visitor Center: 301/497-5760; North Tract Visitor Contact Station: 410/674-3304

TOURING PATUXENT

■ **BY AUTOMOBILE:** A 9-mile Wildlife Loop swings through the center of North Tract. South Tract has no auto-tour route per se, but Scarlet Tanager Loop, the one-way road in and out of the Visitor Center and headquarters, passes through woodlands where wildlife can be seen.

■ **BY FOOT:** There are 13 miles of foot trails in North Tract. Short trails, about 5 miles in total, may be accessed from the Visitor Center.

■ **BY BICYCLE:** North Tract Wildlife Loop and other designated trails are open to bicycles. Check at the Contact Station. No off-road or off-trail biking is allowed.

■ **BY TRAM:** Visiting groups can schedule guided tours on an electric tram (spring through fall) that carries them over dirt roads through a variety of habitats, including forests and wetlands and wildlife management demonstration areas. This is a weekday (seasonal and weather-dependent) activity. The public may ride on a first-come, first-served basis on weekends.

■ **BY HORSE:** Inquire at the North Tract Visitor Contact Station about where horseback riding is currently allowed. Riding is part of the heritage of this property. Stables still stand on land that was formerly part of adjacent Fort Meade, once the key post of the U. S. Cavalry.

WHAT TO SEE

Patuxent is located on the flat landscape of the coastal plain. Most of the refuge is forested. Scattered through the forest are 50 impoundments, beaver flowages, and natural wetlands. The climate is like that of the two cities that it lies between, Baltimore and Washington. Summers at times can be uncomfortably hot and muggy; winters are not brutally cold but can occasionally bring some serious snow; and fine weather is the norm in fall and spring.

■ **PLANT LIFE** To say that Patuxent is "forested" may be an oversimplification. The refuge is rich in plant communities, many of them wetlands with a full spectrum of aquatic and semiaquatic plants. The large number of plant communities, some created by human intervention, make Patuxent a wise choice for wildlife management research and demonstration.

Forest The dominant plant community of Patuxent is deciduous hardwood. Beech are common here, as are a variety of oaks. Coniferous trees include Virginia pine, pitch pine, typical of the northern areas of the coastal plain, shortleaf pine, and loblolly pine, a southern species that is at the northern end of its range.

Marshes, lakes, ponds, and impoundments The vegetation in Patuxent's wetlands varies according to the plants' individual characteristics. However, the shallows of every wetland on the refuge contain soft rush, woolgrass, squarestem spikerush, and eastern bur reed. Among the myriad other wetland plants here are watershield, water lily, bladderwort, and spatterdock. Cattails, rice cutgrass, and millet are common.

Swamps Several species of trees and shrubs grow in seasonal and permanent swamps within the refuge, among them willow oak, white oak, sweet gum, and red maple trees. Shrubs thriving in damp places include ilex, buttonbush, and arrowwood.

■ **ANIMAL LIFE** Patuxent's rich diversity of animal life is due largely to the fact that it is a place where scientists research, test, and demonstrate techniques designed to maintain and improve wildlife habitat. No other refuge in the NWR system receives such intensive attention from researchers and wildlife managers. Knowledge gained here has been used to improve refuges and other wildlands elsewhere and to restore species that were declining.

Birds Patuxent is an undeniable boon for birders: Many of the 231 species recorded here are common all year or at least during predictable periods. An all-year regular is the great blue heron, which generally cannot be seen in more northern states during the winter. Black ducks, which usually also leave the north when the freeze arrives, are found here in every season. Three owls—barred, eastern screech, and great horned—also belong to this group of year-round residents, as do the eastern bluebird and the crow-sized pileated woodpecker, known for its brilliant red crest.

You can view warblers here in spring, summer, and fall. Among them, you might spot the pine, yellowthroat, prairie, and black-throated blue warbler. Both summer and scarlet tanagers enliven Patuxent's woods during the summer. Mallards, black ducks, and Canada geese are seen year-round; wood ducks show up in the summer, and ring-necked ducks winter here. Among raptors, Cooper's and sharp-shinned hawks are common migrants; red-shouldered, red-tailed, and broad-winged hawks are those most frequently seen. Eagles have also nested here for several years.

Mammals Numerous beavers and muskrats ply the waters of

Barn owl

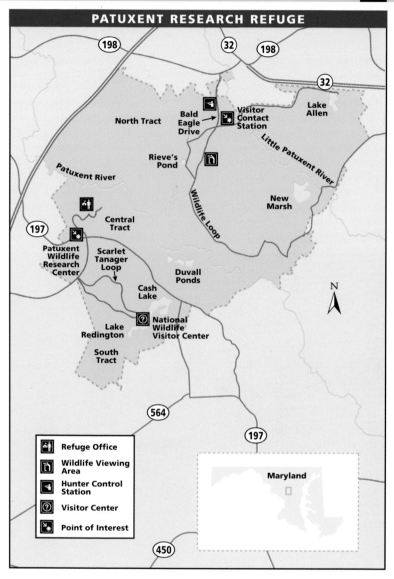

PATUXENT RESEARCH REFUGE

North Tract

Bald Eagle Drive

Visitor Contact Station

Lake Allen

Rieve's Pond

Little Patuxent River

Patuxent River

New Marsh

Wildlife Loop

Central Tract

197

Patuxent Wildlife Research Center

Scarlet Tanager Loop

Duvall Ponds

Cash Lake

National Wildlife Visitor Center

Lake Redington

South Tract

564

197

450

N

Refuge Office

Wildlife Viewing Area

Hunter Control Station

Visitor Center

Point of Interest

Maryland

Patuxent. The beavers are wildlife managers in their own right, creating wetlands that attract waterfowl and provide habitat for fish and amphibians. As beavers cut back woodlands at the water's edge, they open up the land to the growth of browse, favored by white-tailed deer. Otters also live on the refuge. They are not common but may be increasing here.

Both the red fox and gray fox are frequently seen. *Fox* is a term in the general language used to describe a large number of small, wild canids (commonly known as the dog family) that are look-alikes—most have bushy tails and large ears—but are not essentially closely related. The red fox and gray fox, in fact, are only distant cousins. They also differ in behavior. Gray foxes are more likely to be seen by day than are red fox, which are primarily nocturnal. And the gray fox is able to do what few other canids can: It climbs trees, though not with the skill of a cat. When pursued, it often takes refuge in trees. It even hunts for eggs and nestlings in the branches and sometimes eats berries, fruits, and nuts—an important part of its diet—above the ground.

Reptiles and amphibians Some reptile and amphibian species are in decline at Patuxent. Scientists believe that the molesnake and eastern kingsnake are not as common as in the past. The spotted salamander is now scarce in pools where it once massed in spring to reproduce. Other species are thriving here, however. Spring peepers and northern cricket frogs fill the air with their calls in spring. Green frogs are often seen along the edges of streams and impoundments. Black rat snakes, northern water snakes, and blackwater snakes thrive in Patuxent's wetlands. Garter snakes, to the surprise of some people, are almost as aquatic as water snakes. Although garter snakes survive even in the inhospitable habitats of vacant lots in cities, they fare much better in places that have ponds and streams. Fish and other small aquatic creatures are among their favorite fare. Snake fanciers who keep garter snakes as pets sometimes feed them goldfish. Even more of a fine meal to a garter snake is a toad; and the refuge has plenty of American toads.

Box turtle

ACTIVITIES

■ **CAMPING:** Camping is not allowed on the refuge, but camping facilities are available at Patapsco Valley State Park, on Route 40, 20 miles from the refuge.
■ **WILDLIFE OBSERVATION:** An oasis in a heavily urbanized area, Patuxent NWR is a center of intense wildlife and habitat management. The result: Wildlife concentrates here and is easy to see. Wild creatures can be spotted with regularity in any of the areas open to the public. One of the best sites is in North Tract, where the Baltimore Gas and Electric Company helped create a wetland and wildlife-viewing area. Come here to view waterfowl, shorebirds, raptors, and songbirds. The area is a short walk off Wildlife Loop. Nature reigns here now, but this spot was once a testing range for army artillery, when the air echoed to man-made thunder, and the ground shuddered from the impact of explosives.

The Visitor Center in South Tract has an indoor viewing pod—a walk-in glass enclosure—for close-up views of nature. Here, spotting scopes and binoculars are available for use through a large window overlooking wildlife habitat.

■ **EXHIBITS:** The Visitor Center's exhibits are mainly interactive. They include five life-scale habitat areas where visitors can learn, hands-on, how wildlife research has led to important discoveries, and instructive dioramas of imperiled species, such as wolves and whooping cranes. These exhibits focus on global environmental issues, migratory bird studies, habitats, endangered species and the tools used by scientists to conserve the natural world.

■ **PHOTOGRAPHY:** There is an observation tower along Wildlife Loop at the North Tract viewing area. Areas around the Visitor Center lend themselves to photographers who want to shoot pictures of wildlife without having to go deep into a wilderness to do so.

■ **HIKES AND WALKS:** The refuge offers ample hiking opportunities along flat, easy trails of varying distances. Among the 20 miles of trails: Goose Pond Trail (0.2 mile) traverses a forested wetland to Goose Pond. Laurel Trail (0.4 mile) passes through woodlands filled with colorful mountain laurel. Cash Lake Trail (1.4 miles) traces the edge of Cash Lake; visitors will see beaver lodges and many waterfowl species.

■ **SEASONAL EVENTS:** May: International Migratory Bird Day; June: National Fishing Week; October: National Wildlife Refuge Week.

■ **PUBLICATIONS:** Bookshop and gift shop at Visitor Center, with environmental books and educational materials; operated by Friends of Patuxent Wildlife Research Center.

HUNTING AND FISHING There is a wealth of fishing to be had at Patuxent. Species include **smallmouth** and **largemouth bass**, **trout**, **striped bass**, **chain pickerel**, **bluegill**, **catfish**, and **yellow perch**. **American shad** spawns in Patuxent River. In North Tract, visitors can fish Lake Allen, New Marsh, Cattail Pond, Rieves Pond, Bailey Bridge Marsh, and Little Patuxent River. Cash Lake, near the Visitor Center and off Route 197, is usually fished from mid-June to mid-Oct. but has been temporarily drained, so that any fishing activity is pending; call the refuge for further updates.

Patuxent also offers hunting opportunities, including hunting for **white-tailed deer**. A hunting program on North Tract runs from Sept. 1 through Jan. 31; permits are required.

Cape May NWR
Cape May Courthouse, New Jersey

View from Cape May lighthouse, tidal wetlands, Cape May NWR

Although still a fledgling, Cape May NWR has grown from nearly 90 acres at its inception to almost a hundred times that size. The refuge continues to expand toward the U.S. Fish & Wildlife Service's ultimate goal of preserving 16,700 acres of habitat critical to migrating birds on New Jersey's Cape May Peninsula.

The refuge is a patchwork of parcels, many scattered among housing developments that have overtaken 40 percent of lower Cape May Peninsula's migratory bird habitat since 1972. The peninsula's location at the mouth of Delaware Bay makes it a hub for shorebirds migrating north from the tropics in spring. On the shores of Delaware Bay, for example, 80 percent of the Western Hemisphere's red knots—more than 200,000 of them—alight to feed in May and early June. The knots and other shorebirds find lodgings in the refuge's salt marshes and on adjacent beaches. In fall, raptors take a much-needed break at Cape May before crossing Delaware Bay. Cape May's woodlands are a haven for migrating neotropical songbirds, rounding out the region's status as one of the world's birding meccas.

HISTORY

Cape May NWR, established in 1989, is part of a network of preserves, some owned by the state of New Jersey, others by conservation organizations, designed to keep the peninsula hospitable for weary, hungry feathered migrants. A satellite of Edwin B. Forsythe National Wildlife Refuge, 50 miles to the north, near Atlantic City, Cape May refuge has two main sections. Delaware Bay Division is in Middle Township, while Great Cedar Swamp Division is a few miles north, straddling Dennis and Upper Townships.

GETTING THERE

Near the southern terminus of the Garden State Parkway, take Exit 10 and go west for about 1 mi. on Stone Harbor Blvd. At the stoplight on Rte. 9, turn left (south) and proceed for approximately another mi. Turn right (west) at Hand Ave. and follow to the end at Delsea Dr./ Rte. 47. Turn left (south) and go about a hundred yards. On the right is Kimbles Beach Rd. Refuge headquarters is in a small house on the right.

■ **SEASON:** Refuge open year-round.
■ **HOURS:** General refuge: dawn to dusk. Headquarters: 8 a.m.–4 p.m.
■ **FEES:** None.
■ **ADDRESS:** Cape May NWR, 24 Kimbles Beach Rd, Cape May Courthouse, NJ 08210
■ **TELEPHONE:** 609/463-0994

TOURING CAPE MAY

■ **BY AUTOMOBILE:** Motorized vehicles are prohibited on the refuge.
■ **BY FOOT:** Woodcock Trail, a 1.5-mile loop off Rte. 47 less than a mile south of refuge headquarters, is easy walking. It passes through fields and forests and provides entry to a salt marsh.
■ **BY BICYCLE:** Bicycle trails are currenly not available, but should be in the near future.
■ **BY CANOE, KAYAK, OR BOAT:** There are no designated facilities for canoeing or boating on the refuge. However, there are creeks navigable by small boat or canoe.

WHAT TO SEE

■ **LANDSCAPE AND CLIMATE** If the sea level were to rise a few feet, much of Cape May refuge would be the habitat of fish, not birds. This is a refuge that lies low to the ocean. Summers are generally hot and humid, and the infamous Jersey mosquitoes thrive. Spring and fall, however, are delightful, and, as a rule, snowfall in winter is minimal.

■ **PLANT LIFE** Cape May NWR boasts a variety of plant communities, ranging from salt marshes dominated by cordgrasses to upland forest, with pines and oaks. In Great Cedar Swamp, a deep, shadowed forest comprising about half the refuge, Atlantic cedar trees—increasingly rare—rise straight as arrows to the sky.

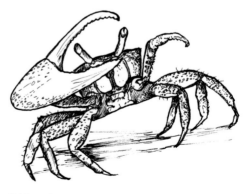

■ **ANIMAL LIFE** Avian life is the main attraction here. Cape May is birders' heaven. The Cape May Peninsula is famous for having the greatest accumulation of raptors in the nation, primarily during the fall.

Fiddler crab

Birds The statistics say it all. There are more than 317 species of birds on this refuge, including more than a dozen raptors, such as peregrine falcons and broad-winged hawks, and about 30 types of warblers. Fall brings an immense concentration of migrating woodcock. They nestle for the day in thickets and moist woodlands, near fields where, mostly at night, they probe for earthworms, often eating their weight of the squiggly creatures between dawn and dusk.

Mammals White-tailed deer are abundant enough to be hunted at Cape May refuge. Many small mammals, including river otters, inhabit the refuge.

Reptiles and amphibians The odds of seeing a rare bog turtle or pine barrens tree frog are low, but both these imperiled species find a haven in the refuge. The eastern box turtle, a declining species, can sometimes be seen.

Invertebrates The hordes of fiddler crabs scuttling about the edge of the marsh along Woodcock Trail are fun to watch. From spring to fall, butterflies abound in Cape May, adding vibrant color to the scene.

ACTIVITIES

■ **WILDLIFE OBSERVATION:** The 1.5-mile Woodcock Trail is good for finding songbirds and, in the salt marsh, wading birds. Reeds Beach, one mile north of the refuge office, is jammed with shorebirds in season. The state of New Jersey operates a public parking lot there.

■ **PHOTOGRAPHY:** Woodcock Trail offers the best opportunities for photography here, but there are no bird blinds or observation towers.

■ **HIKES AND WALKS:** Besides Woodcock Trail, a series of old logging roads through Great Cedar Swamp are used by walkers. Warning: The roads are not well marked or maintained, and it is easy to become confused about direction there. Use a map and a compass, and keep in mind that you're never far from a road.

HUNTING AND FISHING Deer, **waterfowl**, and **woodcock** can be hunted from Oct. through Jan. Sport fish in Delaware Bay include **bluefish**, **fluke**, **stripers**, and **weakfish**. Contact the refuge for more information on exact seasons, permits, and regulations.

■ **PUBLICATIONS:** General refuge brochure and map.

Edwin B. Forsythe NWR
Oceanville, New Jersey

Black skimmers

On a sunny day, the towers of Atlantic City's glitzy gambling palaces just a few miles away lace the horizon. Vividly etched against the blue, the high-rises dominate the view to the southeast across the marshes of Edwin B. Forsythe National Wildlife Refuge. Seen from the vantage point of the refuge wildlife drive, the contrasts are surreal: On one hand are mountains of steel, glass, and concrete, where ice clinks in cocktail glasses and slot machines jingle; an artificial environment that knows neither night nor day, sealed off from the natural elements. On the other are acres of undeveloped marshes, where nature is present in the raw. It's a wild landscape where ocean winds assault the cordgrass at will; where gulls, once airborne, fight to make headway against the wind.

At the edge of the marsh, hunkered down a few feet from roadside, is a peregrine falcon, a hunter that can snatch ducks and other birds out of the air after dives exceeding 200 miles per hour, earning it a reputation as the swiftest bird on earth. Fierce eyes, hooked beak, and wickedly hooked talons strike the peregrine's prey with lethal impact (see sidebar, below).

Visiting the refuge when it's sunny is a pleasant way to spend the day. But a perception of why National Wildlife Refuges exist may, oddly enough, become clearer on a stormy, wind-roiled day. The wildness of this place, tottering on the edge of civilization, is vividly underscored. And it looks like it will stay that way: About 6,000 acres of Forsythe are designated as National Wilderness Area, where the marshes will remain wild and trackless.

HISTORY

This area was not always on the edge of the sea. But it became so about 10,000 years ago, when the sea level rose in response to the meltdown of Ice Age glaciers. Native peoples thrived on the shores of today's southern New Jersey. Their ancestors hunted mammoths, bison, and other big game of the Pleistocene era,

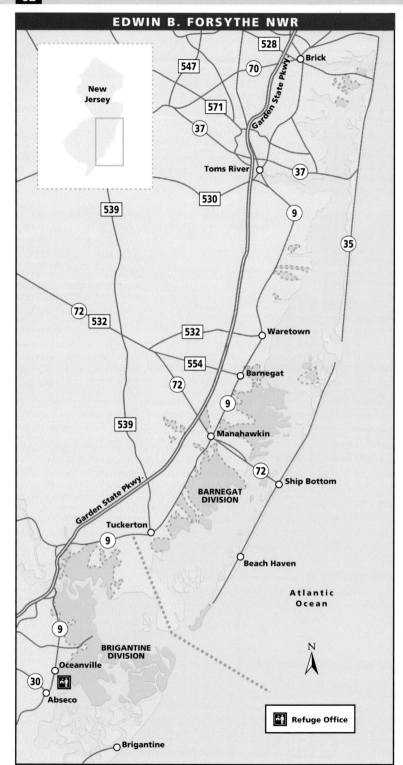

following the migrations of their prey. As the climate warmed and the ocean invaded land, there were fish, clams, crabs, and other fruits of the sea for the taking. So the native people became less nomadic and turned to agriculture, as well as hunting, fishing, and gathering.

By the time of European contact, the primary inhabitants of the area were the Lenape, a band of Algonquians related by language, culture, and blood to many other groups of the northern Middle Atlantic, collectively called the Delawares by the Euro-Americans who eventually displaced them. In one of the dialects of the Delaware tribes, *Lenape* means "real person."

By the early years of the 20th century, the shores on which the Lenape hunted and fished were being transformed by development. Housing, industry, marinas—you name it—replaced marshes, sand beaches, and coastal scrub forest.

Forsythe has two divisions, Barnegat, with little public access, and Brigantine, to the south, the site of the wildlife drive. Both the Brigantine and Barnegat divisions of this refuge were established as distinct units—Brigantine in 1939 and Barnegat in 1967—to protect tidal wetlands and bays behind barrier islands as habitat for migratory water birds. Given the pervasive development of the South Jersey coast, there are precious few places left for migratory birds to rest, winter, and nest. The larger portion of Barnegat is on the mainland shore of the bay of the same name. Brigantine is centered on Great Bay and Little Bay. In 1984, the refuges were combined and named after Edwin Forsythe, the late congressman who fought for conservation causes.

Although Forsythe refuge comprises 43,000 acres, most of it has little or no public access. The prime visitor area here, hosting more than 200,000 people annually, is the wildlife drive, an 8-mile loop beginning next to refuge headquarters at the refuge's Brigantine Division.

GETTING THERE

Headquarters is off Great Creek Rd. in Oceanville, which runs east off Rte. 9. From the south, take Rte. 9 north from Abescon, on the western border of Atlantic City, and turn right. From the north, use Garden State Pkwy. to Exit 48, follow Rte. 9 south and turn left on Great Creek Rd.

■ **SEASON:** Refuge open year-round, with exceptions. The Holgate Unit, at the southern tip of Long Beach Island—which is 18 miles in length—is closed from the beginning of April to the start of Sept. to protect nesting shorebirds.

■ **HOURS:** Refuge public-use areas: sunrise to sunset. Headquarters and Auditorium/Visitor Center: 8 a.m.–4 p.m., weekdays.

■ **FEES:** Wildlife drive and associated short nature trails: $4 per private vehicle. Yearly pass: $12. The few other areas of public access to the refuge are free.

■ **ADDRESS:** Edwin B. Forsythe NWR, Great Creek Rd., P.O. Box 72, Oceanville, NJ 08231

■ **TELEPHONE:** 609/652-1665

TOURING FORSYTHE

■ **BY AUTOMOBILE:** The wildlife drive provides sweeping views of wetlands and Turtle Cove, an offshoot of Great Bay.

■ **BY FOOT:** The refuge discourages walking on the drive; it sends away wildlife. Two foot trails lead off the road, affording wooded strolls with marsh views.

■ **BY BICYCLE:** The refuge discourages bicycles on the wildlife drive.

■ **BY CANOE, KAYAK, OR BOAT:** Many areas of marsh in Forsythe can be reached by channels from launching areas outside the refuge or from Scott's

Landing, within Brigantine Division, at the end of Scott's Landing Rd., off Moss Hill Rd., at Leed's Point.

■ **LANDSCAPE AND CLIMATE** Forsythe NWR lies at the edge of the Middle Atlantic Coastal Plain. It is, in a word, flat. Most of it is below 60 feet in elevation and much of it only a handful of feet above sea level. The refuge consists of 78 percent salt marsh. The rest is a smattering of upland forests and swamps.

Some of the most important habitats in the Brigantine Division are not natural: There are two managed impoundments within the inner perimeter of the wildlife drive, which runs along dikes retaining these two bodies of water. One, the 900-acre West Pool, is freshwater. Separated from it by a dike—not open to the public—is the brackish, 700-acre East Pool. In the spring, water levels are lowered to promote plant growth and feeding habitat for migratory aquatic birds. Mud-flats are exposed, enhancing the vigor of plants. Wildlife viewing improves, too, because shorebirds and waterfowl gather on the slick surfaces of the flats to feed before heading to northern breeding grounds. In the fall, water is allowed to deepen. Waterfowl heading south or birds that winter over here, such as Atlantic brant, have a place to paddle and dabble. Birds also utilize the tidal waters of Turtle Cove, an offshoot of Little Bay, whose waters fringe the outside perimeter of the drive.

Winters in South Jersey can be frigid. Summers, however, can be hot and muggy. After all, were it not for a jog determined by politics, much of southern New Jersey would be below the Mason-Dixon Line, officially in the South. The most severe weather comes in the form of storms blasting in from the sea, usually bringing high winds and pouring rain. Some are so powerful that waves from Turtle Cove have sometimes damaged the dike where the wildlife drive runs.

Peregrine falcon

■ **PLANT LIFE** The plant communities of Forsythe are representative of coastal South Jersey, at least where development has not disturbed them. The vast marshes are the most impressive vegetative sight here. Woodlands tend to be rather scrubby, although their appearance does not detract from their role as important wildlife habitat.

Barrier beaches Forsythe protects two small but precious areas of undeveloped barrier beach, the Holgate Unit, which is open to the public between September and April, and, north of Atlantic City, the island of Little Beach, which is closed to the general public. Holgate can be reached via Route 72 east off the Garden State Parkway. Here rise dunes, endlessly changing under the forces of wind and waves. The dunes, and the biological communities they support, have disappeared from most developed beaches on South Jersey's barrier islands. That is because development has destroyed plants, such as American beach grass, that trap blowing and flowing sand, stabilize the dunes, and bulwark them against wind and water. Although only a fragment of the refuge, these undisturbed barrier beaches are among its true treasures.

Tidal marshes The salt marshes constituting most of the refuge are dominated by two species of cordgrass, the key to the marsh system. Cordgrasses are an indication of water salinity. Salt-marsh cordgrass grows closest to the sea because it can better tolerate high salinity, frequent flooding, and lower ground than salt- meadow cordgrass, which is found mostly on the upland margins of the marshes.

Fresh and brackish marshes Cordgrasses also grow in the refuge's brackish marshes, intermediate between the true salt marsh and inland freshwater marshes, which at Forsythe are largely the result of impoundments. Freshwater marsh is marked by plants such as rushes and sedges and, on hummocks, various shrubs and small trees, including sweet bay magnolia.

Forests About 5,000 acres of the refuge are covered by woodlands, ranging from swampy areas, some of which contain the increasingly rare Atlantic white cedar, to uplands, consisting largely of pitch pine, oaks and, in some places, red cedar. In these woodlands, the glossy green leaves of holly is a frequent sight.

HELPFUL HACKERS The "hacking" tower rising alongside the wildlife auto-tour road at Forsythe refuge stands in testimony to the remarkable success story of how the peregrine falcon was snatched back from the jaws of extinction. During the 1970s, it appeared as if the peregrine might join the dodo as a bird whose like would never be seen again. Pesticides, such as DDT, had invaded the peregrine's reproductive system via the food chain. As a result, the shells of peregrine eggs became so fragile that they often shattered when parent birds tried to incubate them.

Government agencies and nonprofit conservation organizations mounted a last-ditch effort to save the birds. Peregrines were bred in captivity. Eggs were removed from wild nests before they could break and were incubated carefully in the laboratory. Gradually, significant numbers of young were produced.

The next step was to reintroduce them into the wild. One method used was dubbed "hacking." Four-week-old falcons were placed in a box about the size of a typical doghouse and surrounded by bars. Boxes were placed on high places: cliffs and towers, for example. Researchers fed the young using hand puppets that resembled adult peregrines.

After a few weeks, the bars were removed. The young birds began testing their wings, in place at first. Scientists continued to feed them. If all worked well, as it did increasingly, the birds soon fledged and, little by little, peregrines reestablished themselves in the wild. Most remarkably, the birds were recently removed from the federal endangered species list.

■ **ANIMAL LIFE** For the visitor, aquatic birds are the main draw at Forsythe. However, sharp eyes can find other animals as well.

Birds Almost 300 species of birds have been observed at Forsythe, some only occasionally, others in mind-boggling numbers. The marshes are the haunt of rails, a smallish relative of cranes that stalks small crabs and other invertebrates at water's edge. Rails are more often heard than seen because they are experts at staying under the cover of marsh grasses. But their clattering calls can reveal their presence.

During the spring, and also in fall, the shorebirds are here. Rare piping plovers nest on protected beaches. Willets, wings flashing black and white, teem in the impoundments and in Turtle Cove. Spring through summer is the time of wading birds. Great egrets, snowy egrets, great blue herons, and the tricolored heron, considered uncommon, are sometimes spotted.

Spring and, especially, fall bring the most spectacular avian sights to Forsythe. During fall and early winter, the refuge may host more than 180,000 waterfowl. Dark clouds of brant swing through the sky, then alight in marshes to pick up grit and feed on sea lettuce, a common marine alga. Snow geese by the tens of thousands wing in, gorging on the roots of marsh plants, killing them and leaving bare mudflats, called "eat outs," in their wake. Black ducks, gloriously colored gadwalls, and mallards seem to be everywhere.

Raptors, including northern harriers and occasional bald eagles, are frequently noted at Forsythe. The prize among them is the peregrine falcon. More than a thousand peregrines migrate through South Jersey, and some wild peregrines nest here.

Mammals About 40 species of mammals inhabit the refuge. Some, like white-tailed deer and the red fox,

Piping plover

are common here and call Forsythe home year-round. Bats use Forsythe in the same way that many birds do: as a migratory rest stop or wintering area. The need for habitat in a shrinking natural world is as important to the hoary and silver-haired bat as it is to the piping plovers and brant. Other mammals include white-tailed deer, muskrats, cottontail rabbits, and eastern chipmunks.

Reptiles and amphibians The reptiles most commonly seen on Forsythe are turtles: eastern box turtles (population declining quickly) and diamondback terrapins; painted turtles that abound in freshwater; and the ubiquitous snapping turtle. Some of them lay their eggs in the soil of the wildlife drive during the spring, so drivers should keep an eye peeled. Most common of amphibians is the green frog—green as the pondweed among which it often rests in almost every freshwater pond or pool in the refuge.

Invertebrates In May and June, horseshoe crabs breed on the edges of Turtle Cove and the barrier beaches of Forsythe. Their little green eggs serve more than a reproductive purpose. The nutrient rich eggs nourish shorebirds that stop at the refuge during their migration from Central and South America to their breeding grounds near and at the edges of the Arctic Ocean.

ACTIVITIES

■ **WILDLIFE OBSERVATION:** Visitors will want to take in the view from the observation platform built over a 600-acre impoundment in the Barnegat Division, on Bayshore Drive, between Ridgeway and Edison avenues, east of Route 9, in Oceanville, New Jersey.

To see the most wildlife at Forsythe, take the wildlife drive. Stay in your car so that you don't disturb the animals. During the spring, nesting Canada geese and their young are very visible. Look at the West Pool for freshwater birds, such as wood ducks. The East Pool is a great spot for sandpipers. Turtle Cove and salt marshes adjacent to it are neat spots to see brant and snow geese. Uplands near the drive's end support songbirds. There are two observation towers along the drive. One is near the drive's entrance, at the end of Gull Pond Road, a short loop. The other is a short distance down the drive affording a view of the impoundments and Turtle Cove.

■ **PHOTOGRAPHY:** Photographers make use of the towers or simply stop along the drive and shoot through open car windows. Most shots of the cove and salt marshes will be to the west. Since the drive encircles the impoundments, many directional angles are available.

■ **HIKES AND WALKS:** Easy walks at the Brigantine Division include Leeds Eco-Trail, a 0.5-mile loop through salt marsh and woodlands; the salt marsh portions are boardwalked. Akers Woodland Trail runs 0.25 mile through native woodlands and is a good spot for seeing migrating warblers. The only trail in the Barnegat Division is deCamp Wildlife Trail, 1 mile, located at Matoloking and Adamson roads in Brick Township.

■ **SEASONAL EVENTS:** May: International Migratory Bird Day; October (usually the second Saturday): National Wildlife Refuge Week, with a variety of public events, including lectures, tours, and presentations, as well as the reopening of the Visitor Center.

HUNTING AND FISHING There is fishing allowed in the saltwater portions of the refuge, by boat only. You're likely to come back with mainly **flounder** and the occasional **striped bass**. There is also freshwater fishing in Lily Lake, where you will find **walleye** and **bass**. All fishing is year-round.

There are three **deer** hunts on the refuge in the late fall/early winter: archery, muzzle-loader, and shotgun. These seasons run concurrently with the state seasons. There is also a **waterfowl** season that runs from Oct. through Feb. Contact the refuge for exact dates for all of these seasons and for information on permits and restrictions.

■ **PUBLICATIONS:** Refuge brochure, including a calendar of seasonal wildlife activity; a checklist of birds; plus a map of the wildlife drive.

Great Swamp NWR
Basking Ridge, New Jersey

Great Swamp NWR

Stands of virgin timber, with ancient beeches more than a dozen feet around, rise above lush marsh and wild woody swamps. Great blue herons fish in the shallows. Bog turtles, an endangered species, hide in soggy areas. Bluebirds abound. Wild turkey hens shepherd their young through the woods, on guard against the few coyote families that have staked out their territories in the area. During spring and summer the soft night resounds to the beeps of spring peepers, the bellows of bullfrogs, and the calls of green frogs, all here to reproduce their kind.

Great Swamp NWR, currently at 7,500 acres, is an oasis, an island of the wild among the highly developed suburbs of New York City, about 30 miles to the east.

HISTORY

For centuries, the Lenape Indians, a group also known to Euro-Americans as the Delaware, hunted and fished in the swamp. They were displaced by American colonists and removed westward. Land in and around the swamp was logged and farmed; portions of the swamp were wet and wild enough to withstand the pressure for exploitation.

In mid-20th century, suburban sprawl closed in the swamp. A far more serious threat to its integrity loomed, however. In 1959, the Port Authority of New York and New Jersey proposed building a 10,000-acre jetport here, to include land occupied by the swamp, on about the only open area remaining in these parts. The proposal sparked immense public outrage, and the jetport idea was eventually dropped.

In the midst of the controversy, conservationists banded together successfully to defend the swamp. In 1960, Great Swamp NWR was established. Six years later, the refuge was designated a National Natural Landmark. And in 1968 more than 3,600 acres of the swamp was designated as the first National Wilderness Area on

Department of Interior lands. A "National Wilderness" in the suburbs of New York City? That's why Great Swamp refuge is so precious.

GETTING THERE

From New York City, head west on US 80. After about 30 mi., go south for 12 mi. on US 287 to Exit 30A, Basking Ridge/North Maple Ave. Stay on North Maple Ave. to first traffic light and follow refuge directional signs.

■ **SEASON:** Refuge open year-round.

■ **HOURS:** Public areas open dawn–dusk, seven days a week. Headquarters open 8 a.m.–4:30 p.m. year-round Mon.–Sat., as well as some Sundays 11 a.m.–5 p.m. in the spring and fall.

■ **ADDRESS:** 152 Pleasant Plains Rd., Basking Ridge, NJ 07920

■ **TELEPHONE:** 973/425-1222

TOURING GREAT SWAMP

■ **BY AUTOMOBILE:** A mile-and-a-half of the refuge's gravel Pleasant Plains Rd., which is dead-ended, is designated as a car route. Along the way you will find an information kiosk, an overlook, and spotting scopes.

■ **BY FOOT:** Long Hill Rd. leads to a Wildlife Observation Center overlooking a large portion of the refuge that is in an area managed to promote a diversity of habitats. The center is unstaffed but has interpretative displays and two boardwalk trails leading to observation blinds. Wilderness Area trails cover more than 8 miles and are marked with colored dots on trees. Some of the going is not easy, and young children may find these hikes difficult. Boardwalks bridge some streams, but others are not bridged. Wandering off Wilderness Area trails is permitted but advised only for the woods-wise.

■ **BY BICYCLE:** Bikes are permitted only on public roads.

■ **BY CANOE, KAYAK, OR BOAT:** No boating is allowed in Great Swamp.

WHAT TO SEE

■ **LANDSCAPE AND CLIMATE**

This is North Jersey, almost. Winters can be cold but seldom frigid for long. Summers can be hot, hotter yet in the swamp, where biting insects and ticks can be a problem. But Great Swamp has weather tolerable enough at any time of year.

Great Swamp lies in a shallow depression about 7 miles long, which during the last Ice Age was a lake, a stone's throw south of the front of the Ice Age glaciers. On its northern border is a ridge of glacial till, plowed up by the ice and then dropped as the glacier melted. Once the ice retreated, shorelines eroded and the lake gradually filled with sediment, turning the lake into wetlands. Beneath the swamp, under an accumulation of peat, are clays from

Iris

glacial times that prevent drainage of surface waters, which nowadays are supplied by precipitation and several small tributary streams, as well as the Passaic River on the swamp's western border.

■ **PLANT LIFE** More than 600 species of plants, ranging from mighty beeches and oaks to duckweed, a floating aquatic plant as tiny as a pinhead, are found in Great Swamp. Wildflower lovers are in heaven here, with more than 200 species to search for and admire.

Woodlands Woodlands, accessible by trails in the Wilderness Area, vary according to the moisture of the soil. Low-lying areas are covered by red maples, pin oak, and willows. Uplands are the haven of large beeches, oaks, and shagbark hickory. The understory is thick with highbush blueberry and mountain laurel, blooming spectacularly in May and June. In spring, check the ground in these upland areas for the pink lady's slipper, a rare orchid whose blossom combines a yellow "foot" inside a white "slipper."

Marshes In pools, flooded areas, and along languid streams are marshes of cattails and sedges. Irises bloom purple in spring, and pickerelweed provides an almost similar hue in summer. Buttonbush creates thickets on slightly higher, but still wet, ground. Five shallow impoundments are maintained to promote wetland plant species, which in turn attract aquatic birds and other marsh creatures.

Grasslands The refuge has several hundred acres of grasslands maintained by mowing every few years. The grasses provide food and cover for a variety of birds that prefer or require grassland habitats.

■ **ANIMAL LIFE**

At any time of year, but especially from spring to fall, a wide variety of animals can be spotted in Great Swamp. Most of them are birds (over 220 species), but it is not unusual to see a few mammals as well as reptiles and amphibians.

Birds You can see mallards on ponds and streams throughout the metropolitan New York area. However, wood ducks are something else again. The males, at least, are among the most handsome ducks on the continent and are among the most

Wood ducks

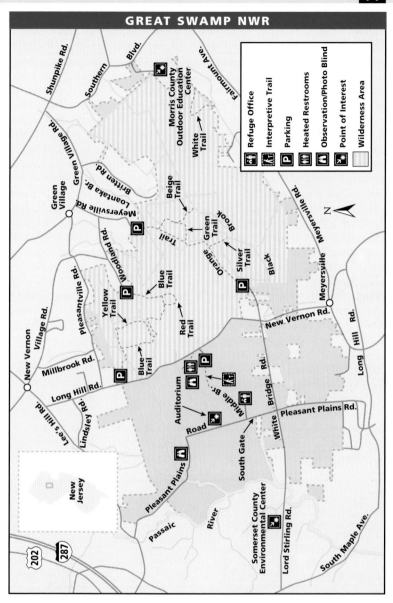

GREAT SWAMP NWR

Legend:
- Refuge Office
- Interpretive Trail
- Parking
- Heated Restrooms
- Observation/Photo Blind
- Point of Interest
- Wilderness Area

N

wary. The wood duck prefers swamps and marshes where trees are abundant. It nests in tree cavities, as well as in boxes provided for it by humans, and is fond of acorns. It is truly a wood duck, and Great Swamp has a population of this species that in spring and summer can number in the thousands, counting young. Of course, mallards, too, are common in the swamp, and other waterfowl, including graceful pintails and Canada geese, are often seen.

Songbirds are here in abundance. Warblers move through in the spring, and, during the nesting season, you will likely see bluebirds in the meadows. This suburban refuge has one of the largest breeding populations of eastern bluebirds in New Jersey. Wading birds, especially the great blue heron, are loath to pass up a well-stocked wetland like this. There are frogs and fish aplenty for the taking. Bobolinks, not as common in the eastern United States as they once were, rise from the grasslands, and wild turkeys roam both grassland and forest. Look for them in the spring, when the males and females gather to mate, and then in the summer, when hens cooperatively herd their young around in large flocks.

Mammals Great Swamp NWR is home to 33 species of mammals. Muskrats populate the marshes, and by eating vegetation and using it to build their lodges, they create openings in the dense emergent marsh vegetation, which benefits waterfowl and other marsh birds. Beaver, once a memory, have returned to the area. They are secretive, but their presence is evident by the stumps of trees that they leave behind. Beaver lodges, large rounded humps of sticks and mud, can usually be seen near the brooks. Look for white-tailed deer feeding at forest and field edges throughout the refuge. One of the finest of all sights is a white-tailed deer standing up to its hocks in water, feeding on aquatic vegetation as its huge relative, the moose, often opts to do. Red foxes abound but are seen only occasionally by day; count yourself lucky if you spot one. These foxes are active all winter, and you may find their tracks in the snow. Raccoons, ultimate survivors of suburban development, are abundant in Great Swamp.

Reptiles and amphibians Of all creatures inhabiting the refuge, reptiles and, especially, amphibians, probably should be most grateful for its creation. Those that live here—39 species—are creatures of quiet and secret places, often the moist and watery spots. The refuge is home to the small, imperiled bog turtle. You probably won't see one, but it is nice to know that this solitary reptile, which has dwindled along with the wetlands that support it, still survives here. Habitats for bog turtles are preciously few.

Snapping turtles are primal creatures, living in much the same way as their ancestors did even before dinosaurs prowled the land. They scavenge as well as prey and seem able to survive almost anything that humanity throws at them. They haunt the waters here and are an intriguing part of the Great Swamp refuge.

In the spring, just as the sun sets, spring peepers will serenade into the night.

Snapping turtle, basking

BOG TURTLE The little bog turtle, with a brown shell less than 5 inches long, is a clandestine creature. It hides in the dark recesses of bogs, seepages, springs, tiny streams, and pools in wet meadows. Although found in southern New England, the heart of its homeland is the mid-Atlantic region. The bog turtle has citadels in the wetlands of New Jersey, Pennsylvania, Delaware, Maryland, and Virginia. Like other small creatures of wetlands, this one also has declined in numbers as the water has been drained or plowed over for real estate development.

Some scientists say that the bog turtle never was common in the region. Some say it is so good at concealing its whereabouts that its numbers are difficult to ascertain. Either way, the bog turtle is not a species that many people see, although in refuges such as the Great Swamp, where bog turtles live, you have a better chance than elsewhere. Look for a small turtle with bright orange spots aside its head; if you get lucky, let the refuge personnel know of your find. It means that you have seen something rare and precious and a good reason why national wildlife refuges exist.

They are so small that one could sit on your thumbnail. And they keep to themselves, hiding their tiny bodies as well as they reveal their locations by their songs. In summer, look for bigger frogs, bullfrogs and green frogs, in the shallows. They float on the water, often among duckweed, and their bulging eyes reveal their presence.

ACTIVITIES

■ **CAMPING:** There is no camping on the refuge. The nearest camping is at one of the New Jersey State Parks; the closest that allows camping is 30 miles away. Contact the refuge for information.

■ **WILDLIFE OBSERVATION:** Great Swamp NWR headquarters provides slide shows and tours for groups. Although Great Swamp refuge lacks a staffed Visitor Center, there are three separate facilities on or adjacent to the refuge that provide many activities for visitors.

Within the refuge, but on private land, is The Raptor Trust, which rehabilitates all species of birds. It has birds on display and offers programs. Morris County operates the Great Swamp Outdoor Education Center next to the refuge. The center has a library, natural history displays, and programs on nature and the environment. Just across the Passaic River from the refuge is Somerset County's Environmental Education Center, with workshops and special events.

Other good places on this refuge for wildlife viewing include Pleasant Plains Road and its overlook, where you have a good chance of sighting a substantial number of wildlife species. Keep an eye out for bluebirds here; this is one of the areas in the refuge they favor. Contrary to popular belief, eastern bluebirds do not always migrate south in winter from the northern tier of states. Many remain during the cold months, often gathering in flocks. Winter, in fact, can be a productive time to look for them. Young bluebirds are actually brownish and drab, often mistaken for sparrows. Pleasant Plains Road is also a fine place to look for great blue herons, deer, and wild turkeys.

The Wildlife Observation Center, on the western side of Long Hill Road, gives boardwalk access into the refuge's management area. Look for waterfowl, especially wood ducks. Perhaps you may see a ribbon snake or water snake winding through the water in search of fish or frogs. The Wilderness Area is on the eastern side of the road. In the wilderness, it is catch as catch can. Wild animals are not as obvious as they are in areas where observation sites have been established. But you may see a beaver sculling through the water or a barred owl perching on a branch. Barred owls are one of the few owl species often seen by day, especially on cloudy days—they enjoy cloudy weather and are more likely to be out and about.

■ **PHOTOGRAPHY:** The Wildlife Observation Center has blinds and provides an excellent overview of wetlands. (Bonus: restrooms are located there.) Otherwise, keep your camera ready along the auto route.

■ **HIKES AND WALKS:** Casual visitors may walk over ponds and wetlands on boardwalk loops—one is 0.5 mile, the other only 0.25 mile—starting from the Wildlife Observation Center through red maple swamp. It's easy going.

For more vigorous hiking, pick up a map at headquarters, bring a compass, then head off Long Hill Road into the Wilderness Area. Remember that, despite its suburban location, this part of Great Swamp is very definitely a wilderness. Except in the driest of periods, waterproof boots are a good idea.

HUNTING AND FISHING The refuge hosts a limited 4-day shotgun and muzzle-loader **deer** hunt in the first week of Dec. Interested hunters should apply through the special permit division of the state of New Jersey gaming department.

There is no fishing allowed on the refuge.

■ **PUBLICATIONS:** At refuge headquarters, various pamphlets on trails and wildlife in Great Swamp.

Wallkill River NWR
Sussex, New Jersey

Wallkill River floodplain, Wallkill River NWR

Where is the real New Jersey? The "Jersey Turnpike," glutted with traffic? The tangled web of bridges and tunnels leading to the Big Apple? A suburb scarred by urban blight and inhabited by commuters whose sylvan backyards were created by bulldozers and landscapers? Many wrongly perceive New Jersey as little more than a somber urban landscape, difficult to admire. But Jersey wasn't dubbed the Garden State for nothing. The Jersey Shore has some of the Northeast's cleanest beaches, and the few remaining tracts of wild coastal lands are protected by national wildlife refuges, the state, and conservation organizations. But too often forgotten is the northwestern corner of New Jersey, a hilly place of dense woods that could almost pass for wilderness. Black bears shamble through the forest, mink prowl stream edges, and a bald eagle occasionally soars overhead.

Here, where New Jersey, New York, and Pennsylvania meet, about 60 miles from the twin towers of the World Trade Center and a quick ride from Patterson or Newark, lies Wallkill River NWR. Cradled by low mountains, the refuge, which lies in New York as well as the Garden State, protects the bottomlands of the Wallkill River floodplain, one of the few large areas of habitat for waterfowl remaining in northwestern New Jersey.

HISTORY

Native Americans called the Wallkill River area *Twischsawkin* ("the place of plums"). For hunters, the valley was an important source of flint and chert for projectile points. Dutch settlers (in Dutch, *kill* means "river or stream"), who spread into the region in early Colonial times, called it "The Drowned Lands," in reference to the seasonal flooding of the bottomlands. During the 19th century, flooding became a political issue. Millers, known as "The Beavers," wanted flooding to continue. Farmers, "The Muskrats," wanted the river controlled to keep agricultural land moist but above water. The farmers won, and the water table of the river was lowered.

The Wallkill River Valley lies astride two major corridors used by waterfowl and other migratory birds—the valleys of the Delaware and Hudson rivers. To preserve part of the valley, with its wetlands and watershed, Wallkill NWR was established in 1990. It began with modest acreage, reached 4,226 acres in 1999, and eventually may cover 7,500 acres. If you visit, be sure to visit the refuge office. Community service workers and volunteers helped renovate a 160-year-old farmhouse with original wood floors and banisters and turned it into a beautiful Visitor Center.

GETTING THERE

The refuge office is at 1547 County Rte. 565. Off Rte. 23, head north on Rte. 565 for a 1.5 mi. Signs direct you to the refuge headquarters.
■ **HOURS:** Visitor Center open 8 a.m.–4:30 p.m., weekdays. Trails open sunrise to sunset.
■ **FEES:** None.
■ **ADDRESS:** Wallkill NWR, 1547 County Rte. 565, Sussex, NJ 07461
■ **TELEPHONE:** 973/702-7266

TOURING WALLKILL

■ **BY AUTOMOBILE:** There is no auto-tour route on this refuge.
■ **BY FOOT:** Two walking trails, offering about 5 miles of footpaths, are open.
■ **BY BICYCLE:** No biking is allowed on this refuge.
■ **BY CANOE, KAYAK, OR BOAT:** The best way to see Wallkill refuge is by canoe. But be prepared to haul your canoe over beaver dams and downed timber. There are three access points: Bassets Bridge, off Rte. 642; Oil City Rd. (east side), off Rte. 88, in Orange County, NY; and Rte. 565, in Sussex, 1 mile from the refuge headquarters.

WHAT TO SEE

■ **LANDSCAPE AND CLI-MATE** West of the valley lie the Kittatinny Mountains, a gentle range of the ridge-and-valley Appalachians. To the east are the Hudson Highlands. Winters can be cold and snowy here, while summer can be warm and humid on some days, delightful on others. The fierce greenhead flies and salt-marsh mosquitoes that make summers difficult in southern

Bullfrog

New Jersey are not found on the refuge. Spring and fall are the best times to visit, however.

■ **PLANT LIFE**
Marshes Throughout the refuge are typical freshwater marshes, with cattails and pickerelweed in the shallows. A green carpet of duckweed covers quiet waters. Some dikes, built by farmers, have been opened to allow a more natural flow of waters. Formerly cultivated black-dirt fields are returning to their wild state.
Wet forests Trees tolerant of seasonal flooding dominate this low-lying plant

community. Species include silver maple, red maple, willow, and, on the edges, sweet gum.

Upland forests Wallkill's hardwood forest is a shadowy place consisting mostly of sugar maple, white oak, and red oak.

Grasslands The refuge staff work with local farmers to maintain former hay-fields. They have also restored over 50 acres of mature, warm-season grasses next to the refuge office. These restored grasslands benefit nesting grassland birds.

■ **ANIMAL LIFE** In the wetlands, forests, and fields of Wallkill River refuge, visitors have a chance to spot more than 225 species of birds, plus several species of mammals.

Birds Black ducks, wood ducks, and mallards use the refuge both during migrations and for nesting. Another important nester is the great blue heron; you might find one fishing at water's edge, standing tall and very still on reedlike legs. Meadows provide nesting for grassland birds, such as bobolinks and savannah sparrows. Spring and fall bring large numbers of hawks and migratory songbirds. A sharp eye, or ear, may spot barred owls in the forest and short-eared owls in the grasslands.

Mammals Wallkill has a rich mammalian fauna, including beaver, muskrats, red and gray foxes, white-tailed deer, and coyotes—plus an increasing number of black bears. You might hear the coyotes calling, if you're on the refuge early or late. The bears should be admired from afar; don't feed them anything. Also present are river otters and their relatives, mink.

Reptiles and amphibians A canoe trip along the river can easily bring a visitor into contact with painted turtles basking on logs. As the weather warms during late spring, male bullfrogs and green frogs take up their calling stations, seeking to attract mates. The bog turtle, on the federal threatened species list, is found on and near the refuge.

> **HUNTING AND FISHING**
> **White-tailed deer** season runs Sept. through Jan., and **wild turkey** can be hunted in April and May. The season varies for hunting resident **Canada geese**.
>   Sport fish include **largemouth bass, pickerel,** and **panfish**.

ACTIVITIES

■ **PHOTOGRAPHY:** Some of the best photo opportunities at Wallkill can be had from a canoe or kayak. Also, a photography blind is located on Wood Duck Nature Trail.

■ **HIKES AND WALKS:** Both refuge trails are easily walked. Wood Duck Nature Trail was built by volunteers and covers 1.5 miles on an abandoned railroad bed. It has benches and a boardwalk across a small stream, Beaver Run, and ends at the Wallkill River.

   Liberty Loop (2.5 miles, some of it on a dike through a former sod farm) encircles a wetland and meadow, a fine place to see waterfowl and grassland birds. This trail is also a section of the Appalachian Trail; Wallkill River NWR is the only national wildlife refuge that includes part of this grand path through the wilderness.

■ **PUBLICATIONS:** Refuge brochure and bird list.

Iroquois NWR
Basom, New York

White water lily

Iroquois NWR, halfway between Rochester and Buffalo in western New York State, bears a proud name. The Iroquois Confederacy, a group of five related tribes that formed a league of Five Nations in the 15th century and were joined by a sixth in the early 1700s, was one of the best-organized and most aggressive Indian groups north of the Mexican border. From their homeland, which stretched across central New York State, they exerted their influence by war club and trade as far west as the Mississippi River and south to Tennessee. Europeans referred to them as the "Romans of the New World."

The refuge's major attraction—but by no means the only one—is the American bald eagle. Visitors throng to Iroquois to see this regal-looking bird, which thrives in the well-preserved wetlands and forests of the refuge. At Iroquois eagles have large trees in which to nest and vast expanses of water where they can hunt for or scavenge fish, their favorite food. The water also attracts a host of other birds: waterfowl by the thousands, a rare tern of unusual beauty, and a small warbler that glistens like gold among the woods.

HISTORY

Like Montezuma NWR to the east in New York, Iroquois contains an abundance of wetlands. These marshes and swamps owe their origin to the last, or Wisconsin, Ice Age. As glaciers covering the region melted northward, water dripped from them to create a large lake; the Native Americans called it Tonawanda. But the lake gradually filled with sediment and became wetlands. Deciduous trees sprouted on surrounding uplands. The shape of the land as we know it today emerged.

Seneca Indians, the westernmost group of Iroquois and the "keepers of the western gate," farmed corn and pumpkins in small plots cut out among the trees. Euro-American settlers, who poured into the area after the Revolution, changed the landscape dramatically after the Iroquois had been reduced by war and disease. Timbering and draining for agriculture took their toll. The most impenetrable of the wild lands, the swampy watershed of Oak Orchard Creek, survived, partly because of underlying rock, which thwarted efforts to siphon off water.

Iroquois refuge, almost 11,000 acres, was established in 1958 to protect these sections, which are extremely important to waterfowl. Two state-owned wildlife management areas border the refuge, one on the east, the other on the west, creating in total 20,000 acres of wild land known as the Alabama Swamp Complex.

Originally, the entire area was known as the Ga-Swa-Deh: "By-the-Cedar Swamp." Settlers, however, noted that the Senecas had left groves of oak trees standing among the farm plots. (This was by design. Acorns were used for food by the Indians as well as by deer and wild turkeys that the Senecas hunted.) To settlers, the oak stands resembled orchards. To locals, the area, including the NWR and the management areas, was generally referred to as Oak Orchard Swamp. More recently, and today still, it is referred to as the Alabama Swamps. "Alabama" is a derivation of an Iroquois word meaning "here we rest."

During the early 1980s, 42 bald eagles were released near the refuge, as part of a national program to restore the species. Two of the eaglets, upon maturity, erected a nest on the refuge in 1986. The male followed suit the next year with a new female. There is no guarantee that there will be a pair of nesting eagles each year, and two nests for the size of the territory is about proper. As a rule, however, eagles have nested on the refuge every year since the first nest was put together, branch by branch, stick by stick.

GETTING THERE:

Iroquois is located about 30 mi. northeast of Buffalo. From the New York State Thruway take Exit 48A in Pembroke. Follow NY 77 north. After about 3 mi. it joins NY 63. Continue to Alabama, follow NY 63 north for 0.75 mi., and turn left to go 1 mi. on Casey Rd. to refuge headquarters.

■ **SEASON:** Refuge open year-round. However, to reduce wildlife disturbance between March 1 and July 14, only designated trails are open for foot travel.

■ **HOURS:** General refuge: sunrise to sunset. Headquarters and Visitor Center: 7:30 a.m.–4 p.m. During spring and fall, depending on availability of volunteers to staff the center, it is sometimes open on weekends.

■ **FEES:** None.

■ **ADDRESS:** Iroquois NWR, 1101 Casey Rd., Basom, NY 14013

■ **TELEPHONE:** 716/948-5445

TOURING IROQUOIS

■ **BY AUTOMOBILE:** There is no designated auto drive in Iroquois refuge.

However, public roads around its perimeter pass by most of the major habitat types within the refuge. There are four overlooks with parking where visitors can view the landscape and wildlife.

■ **BY FOOT:** With the exception of the March 1–July 14 time period, the entire refuge is open to foot travel. This may change in the future. Visitors should check at headquarters about hiking safely off designated trails. The refuge maintains three short designated trails and offers other options for walkers, including roads and dikes.

■ **BY BICYCLE:** Cyclists can use the Feeder Rd.

■ **BY CANOE, KAYAK, OR BOAT:** Portions of Oak Orchard Creek are open to boating, but motors are not allowed. The creek is not easy going. Fallen logs and other obstructions often block the way. Deep mud can be difficult or even

IROQUOIS NWR

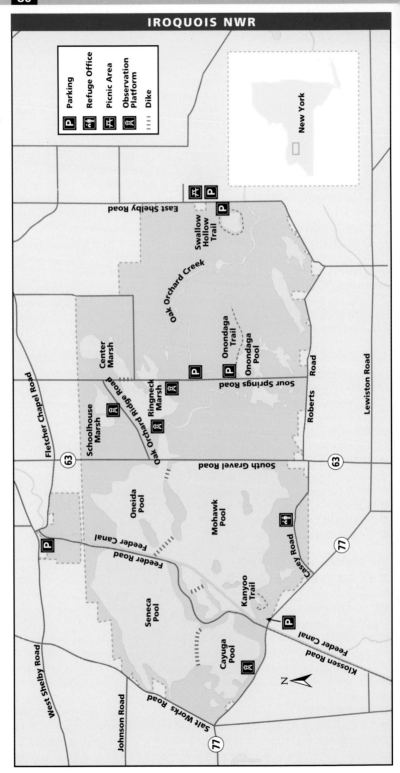

Legend:
- P — Parking
- Refuge Office
- Picnic Area
- Observation Platform
- Dike

New York

East Shelby Road
Swallow Hollow Trail
Oak Orchard Creek
Onondaga Trail
Onondaga Pool
Sour Springs Road
Center Marsh
Ringneck Marsh
Schoolhouse Marsh
Oak Orchard Ridge Road
Fletcher Chapel Road
Roberts Road
Lewiston Road
South Gravel Road
Oneida Pool
Mohawk Pool
Feeder Canal
Feeder Road
Casey Road
Kanyoo Trail
Seneca Pool
Cayuga Pool
Feeder Canal
Klossen Road
Salt Works Road
West Shelby Road
Johnson Road

63
77
N

dangerous during portages. Check refuge headquarters before venturing out. Watercraft may be launched along Knowlesville and Sour Springs roads.

WHAT TO SEE

■ **LANDSCAPE AND CLIMATE** The refuge terrain is generally flat and gentle, with scattered rolling hills covered by hardwood forests. When settlers first arrived from the East, most of the area was quite wet. Drainage projects in the 1800s, however, reduced the wetlands, converting them for agriculture. The land lost much of its ability to hold water. Runoff surged into Oak Orchard Creek, which carried the water to Lake Ontario instead of depositing it in swamps and marshes. Today, most of the remaining wetlands in the refuge would not hold standing water from April through November without human help. In an effort to restore the original hydrological character of the area, refuge dikes and dams contain water year-round, in 16 impoundments, at controlled depths. The result is in improved habitat for wildlife.

Unlike the terrain, the climate can be harsh. Winters in this part of New York State see temperatures often descending below zero and heavy snows. The refuge experiences the brunt of notorious lake-effect snows, which wallop areas on the southern and eastern edges of the Great Lakes. Lake Ontario is about 20 miles north of Iroquois, Lake Erie about

Dragonfly

50 miles west. Erie gives birth to most of the snow here, at least 60 inches in an average year.

■ **PLANT LIFE** Most of Iroquois, approximately 6,200 acres, is marsh. There are also large areas of grasslands plus a scattering of wet meadows and woodlands of trees that can tolerate soggy conditions. Wildflowers bloom in the spring and summer; you are likely to see asters, chickory, and trillium from the footpaths.

Marshes The marshes at Iroquois classify as emergent. Here, water levels remain high enough to prevent the growth of trees and shrubs, and deep enough to allow aquatic plants to prosper. It is a matter of sunlight. If the water is sufficiently shallow for sunlight to penetrate to the bottom—clarity determines the necessary depth—each spring will bring the growth of emergent aquatic vegetation. Cattails, burr reed, sedges, and rushes raise their heads with the coming of spring light and warmth. The marshes at Iroquois are managed to keep water at a level where this annual growth will occur and to prevent marsh from filling in and becoming higher ground.

Forests The woodlands at Iroquois are dominated by red maple. This maple is not as regal as some of its relatives, such the sugar maple, but it can survive swampy conditions that many other maples cannot. Scattered about the woodlands are cottonwoods, which also seek wet places. On higher ground grow some beech, hickories, and even a handful of sugar maples (more characteristic of upland New England).

■ ANIMAL LIFE

Birds Among the great spectacles at Iroquois are skies filled with waterfowl and sightings of bald eagles. These sights are easy to see, in season. Hardcore birders, however, come here for the opportunity to see another species, a small, yellowish bird that nests in the cavities of trees near or overhanging the water, the prothonotary warbler. Less than 5 inches long, it has wings of bluish gray and a golden head and chest. The gold plumage of females tends to be more yellowish than that of the male. It depends on streams and wetlands, where trees are abundant, for habitat. Older trees with cavities are at a premium. Wetlands have been damaged or eliminated. And so, this warbler has declined. But along Oak Orchard Creek, it nests and rears its young, to the delight of birders who can find it.

All told, more than 266 species of birds have been recorded at the refuge.

Eastern cottontail rabbit

These include Canada geese, snow geese, and 24 species of ducks, including wood ducks, mallards, and blue-winged teal. In the refuge and the adjacent state management areas nests the black tern, a graceful bird with sooty plumage. This is the eastern margin of the black tern's breeding grounds.

Mammals Most of the mammals at Iroquois are furtive species. But you stand a good chance of seeing a cottontail rabbit, a white-tailed deer, or a red fox. Muskrats ply the marshes and build their huts of vegetation in the shallows. Beavers build their lodges on the refuge creeks. They are largely active by night, so are not easy to see. But you can see their lodges and dams of sticks and mud, as well as tree stumps that have been gnawed into sharpened points. Raccoons and Virginia opossums go on the prowl in the night.

Reptiles and amphibians In so rich a wetland, aquatic reptiles and amphibians are bound to be common. Snapping turtles lurk in the dark waters. Painted turtles bask on logs and rocks. Northern water snakes slide through the waters, searching for fish and frogs. However, it is in wet meadows rather than open water that the amphibian mostly likely to be seen by visitors lives. This is the

Prothonotary warbler

northern leopard frog, whose skin is covered with bronze spots. After breeding in ponds, pools, and ditches during the spring, leopard frogs fan out into terrestrial, but damp, environments. They are not always common and generally secretive. But a walk through an Iroquois meadow could turn up, in the words of a refuge staffer, "a ton of them." Look down toward the footpath for a small frog leaping away, like a sprite of the meadow.

ACTIVITIES

■ **WILDLIFE OBSERVATION:** The margins of Oak Orchard Creek, accessible by Swallow Hollow and Onondaga trails, are a favorite nesting spot for prothonotary warblers. May is the best time to see warblers at the refuge. Along Route 77 is the large impoundment called Cayuga Pool (the Cayuga were an Iroquois Confeeracy tribe). Located on the western rim of the refuge, the overlook at this pool provides a view of several thousand acres of marshland. Here, black terns swirl and swoop through the air. Early April is the time to see the most Canada geese, numbering upwards of 20,000, sometimes twice that. Spring is always a good time for ducks, although more of them come during early fall, on their southward migration. Ducks sit on the water: redhead, gadwall, and sometimes northern shovelers.

Around the headquarters, bald eagles, purple martins, and bluebirds are often seen. In recent years there have been two eagle nests (which were both used by the one existing pair of eagles), but at present there is only one. Refuge workers have installed video cameras close to the eagles' nest. As long as eagles are nesting here, visitors can view the great birds incubating their eggs and caring for their young on a monitor in headquarters. Viewing usually begins in February and lasts through early summer.

■ **PHOTOGRAPHY:** The refuge has one photo blind. Permits for use of the blind must be obtained at headquarters. It is a good idea to check ahead of time. Many of the other areas in the refuge provide good sites for photography, especially overlooks, such as the one at Cayuga Pool.

IROQUOIS HUNTING AND FISHING SEASONS

Hunting
(Seasons may vary)

	Jan	Feb	Mar	Apr	May	Jun	Jul	Aug	Sep	Oct	Nov	Dec
white-tailed deer										■	■	■
grouse	■	■								■	■	■
rabbits	■	■								■	■	■
gray squirrel	■	■								■	■	■

There is a special wild turkey hunt in the spring. Please note that there are special refuge regulations that apply to hunting on the refuge lands, in addition to New York State regulations. Contact the refuge for details, as well as for more information on the current hunting and fishing license requirements, seasons, and bag limits.

Bank fishing is productive on the refuge, yielding high numbers of largemouth bass, pickerel, yellow perch, bullheads, and bluegills.

■ **HIKES AND WALKS:** The trails maintained by the refuge bring visitors within easy reach of wildlife and key habitats. Choose from Onondaga Trail (1.2-miles one-way), Swallow Hollow Trail (a 1-mile loop with a boardwalk), or Kanyoo Trail (2 loops: .65-mile or 1-mile round-trip). Note: Swallow Hollow's boardwalk is aging. Check with headquarters before using it. Walking is also permitted on the 3-mile Feeder Rd. that runs atop the dike separating the four main impoundments at the refuge.

Walking the roads along the edge of the refuge is also an extremely productive way to see wildlife. The vistas, in many cases, are grander than those on interior trails. The nearby state wildlife management areas also have many trails.

■ **CROSS-COUNTRY SKIING:** The refuge has an 8-mile trail for cross-country skiers that winds through upland forest and fields. Kanyoo and Onondaga trails are also open for skiing and snowshoeing.

■ **PUBLICATIONS:** Maps, checklists of wildlife in the refuge, and descriptions of habitats.

Montezuma NWR
Seneca Falls, New York

Northern shoveler

Before the turn of the 20th century, vast marshes and wetlands lying on what is now Montezuma NWR supported immense numbers of waterfowl. In the early 1900s, these lands were largely drained to facilitate the construction of the Erie Canal. Lush aquatic pastures became mucky fields, conducive to agriculture but hardly so to ducks and geese.

Today, drivers on the New York State Thruway, which bisects the refuge, can glance out either side of their vehicles and see marshland, verdant in spring and summer, brown in fall and winter, stretching to both horizons. The marshes and other wetlands covering most of the refuge's approximately 7,000 acres have been restored by means of an elaborate water-control system using dikes, dams, and locks. The state of New York, Ducks Unlimited, and other conservation organizations worked to restore thousands of additional acres of wetlands adjacent to the refuge.

The New York chapter of the National Audubon Society recognized what is called the Montezuma Complex as its first Important Bird Area in New York. Especially during the fall migratory season, upwards of a million waterfowl descend on Montezuma NWR, which lies in upstate New York, 35 miles of west of Syracuse, and other reserves on its environs, covering pools, clouding the sky, and filling the air with birdsong.

HISTORY

Peter Clark, a wealthy New York City physician, was evidently a well-traveled man. In 1806, when he purchased land and built a home at the northern end of Cayuga Lake, one of New York's five Finger Lakes, he named his estate Montezuma. Clark had taken a fancy to the name, that of the last Aztec ruler, while on a visit to Mexico. The name eventually became attached to the entire area, including the marshes.

Clark was attracted to the area by salt deposits in some of the marshes, which was mined at the time but never became a thriving industry. The Montezuma marshes were watered by overflow from Cayuga Lake, its waters spilling over the banks of the Seneca River. The Cayuga and Seneca people were Indian tribes in the Iroquois Confederacy, resident in the area when Euro-Americans first arrived. Earlier, other Native American groups had taken advantage of the marsh resources but were displaced by the Iroquois.

Although some of the marshes were drained so that their rich muck could be farmed, most remained relatively intact until 1910, when a dam was built at the northern end of the lake and the Seneca River was channelized into a barge canal. Water levels in the wetlands dropped by 10 feet, virtually destroying them as one of the most productive habitats for waterfowl in North America. What had been marshes 12 miles long and 8 miles wide almost disappeared.

The marshes would be resurrected under Franklin Delano Roosevelt's New Deal. In 1937, the federal government purchased almost 7,000 acres of the old marsh, and the refuge was established there the following year. The Civilian Conservation Corps built more than six miles of dikes to create the refuge's two largest impoundments the 1,200-acre Main Pool and Tschache Pool, covering 1,100 acres. Today,

Red fox

water levels are manipulated to reproduce natural seasonal flows beneficial to wildlife. Occasionally, however, nature demonstrates that humans can carry manipulation only so far. Prolonged bouts of wet weather cause Cayuga Lake to flood, sending water surging into the Main Pool, as if to evoke memories of the way things were before people altered natural water systems.

GETTING THERE

From the New York State Thruway, east or west, take Exit 41. Turn right and go south on NY 414 for 200 yards. At the traffic light turn left and go east on NY 318 for 5 mi. NY 318 ends at NY 5 and NY 20, which coincide. Turn left and head east for 1.25 mi. The refuge entrance is on the left.

■ **SEASON:** Refuge open year-round.

■ **HOURS:** Refuge: dawn to dusk. Headquarters: 7:30 a.m.–4 p.m., weekdays. Visitor Center: 10 a.m.–3 p.m., weekdays; 10 a.m.–4 p.m., weekends; March–Nov.

■ **FEES:** None.

■ **ADDRESS:** Montezuma NWR, 3395 Rtes. 5 and 20 East, Seneca Falls, NY 13148

■ **TELEPHONE:** 315/568-5987

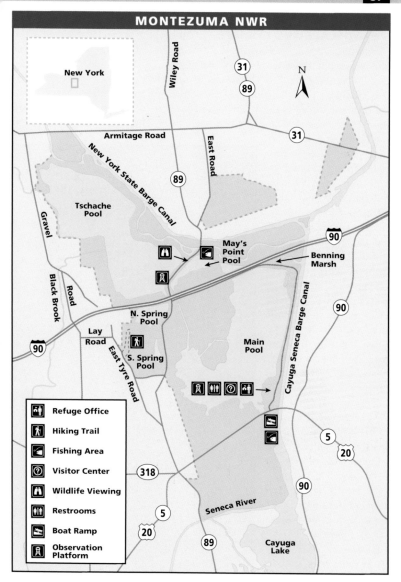

MONTEZUMA NWR

Legend:
- Refuge Office
- Hiking Trail
- Fishing Area
- Visitor Center
- Wildlife Viewing
- Restrooms
- Boat Ramp
- Observation Platform

TOURING MONTEZUMA

■ **BY AUTOMOBILE:** The wildlife drive draws the most visitors to the refuge. Covering 3.5 miles, the drive starts at the Visitor Center. It skirts the Main Pool and the Barge Canal and ends at the Tschache Pool. The drive is not plowed in winter, so is usually not accessible for vehicles.

■ **BY FOOT:** A complex of three trails provides good walking options through various habitats. Woodland views mix with views over the expansive marshes. The wildlife drive is also open to walkers but only in the winter, when the drive is closed to vehicles.

■ **BY BICYCLE:** No biking is allowed on the refuge.

■ **BY CANOE, KAYAK, OR BOAT:** No boating is allowed on the refuge.

WHAT TO SEE

■ **LANDSCAPE AND CLIMATE** The landscape of the region that cradles the Montezuma marshes was born of the Wisconsin Ice Age glaciers as they melted and retreated northward more than 10,000 years ago. Water filled glacial valleys, creating the Finger Lakes. The terrain of the refuge is generally flat. However, there are many ridgelike geologic features that rise above the marshes; they are the final handiwork of the melting glaciers. Lying parallel to one another amid the flats are what appear to be beached whales. They are drumlins: elliptical, rounded hills, usually no more than 100 feet in altitude. Geologists differ on how they were formed, but they were obviously streamlined by water, frozen and liquid, and contain the gritty droppings of rocks and soil from the aging ice. Eskers resemble, to the average person's eye, skinny drumlins—they are longer, with sides that can be almost sheer, but with rounded tops. They appear to have been shaped by water flowing through retreating glaciers.

The climate in this part of New York is far from moderate. During the summer, it can be as hot as it is in the concrete canyons of New York City. Winter brings frigid temperatures and heavy, lake-effect snows off nearby Lake Ontario. Fortunately, the times when wildlife viewing is best, spring and fall, feature weather that is delightful.

Purple loosestrife, Montezuma NWR

■ **PLANT LIFE** Although most of Montezuma refuge is open marsh, several other plant communities can be found here. On the eskers and drumlins there is upland forest. Near Cayuga Lake is a large stand of woody swamp. The refuge also has managed grasslands. The marshes, however, are its hallmark.

Marshes Although the composition of plant species is different, the vista along the New York State Thruway in Montezuma refuge resembles that along Alligator Alley, the highway that carries drivers through Florida's Everglades—not a sea of sawgrass but, nevertheless, similar. Bending and waving in the breeze at

BEAUTIFUL ENEMY It is undeniably gorgeous, with flowers of deep purple. It covers many of the marshes in Montezuma and has been the subject of countless photographs by visitors. But the beauty of purple loosestrife is a mask, at least in this part of the world. A Eurasian species that was introduced into North America during the early 1800s, purple loosestrife is a destroyer. It can bring death to our marshes. It has invaded the refuge, crowding out native plants.

Talk about alien incursions. Purple loosestrife, in botanical terms, is the stuff of scary science fiction. It thrives in wet habitats disturbed by drainage and earth-moving machines. Once settled in, it mass reproduces. A single plant, only a few years old, can generate more than a million seeds. The plants that result are useless to our wildlife. Muskrats do not eat them or use their stiff stems for building lodges. The rugged clumps of loosestrife are too thick to provide cover for nesting waterfowl. And they seem indestructible, lasting for years, trapping sediment and raising the level of land, pushing away the water, in a marsh, working against native plant species.

The war against loosestrife at Montezuma has thus far been a losing one. Herbicides will kill the stuff but also wipe out desirable native plants. So managers have brought in a new weapon—a Fifth Column, so to speak. Beetles and weevils from the Old World, which feed on loosestrife, have been introduced into the area. In 1999, the refuge announced that these insects had survived the frigid winters and were beginning to reproduce. Hopefully, they will be gluttons for loosestrife. But will they find native plants to their liking as well? That is the unanswered question.

Montezuma are thousands of stalks of marsh vegetation, many bearing crowns of flowers or seed heads. Rushes, sedges, and cattails stand tall, in ranks that seem impenetrable. Like so many parts of the Everglades, the marshes of Montezuma are dependent on human management of water that no longer goes with the natural flow. Even so, they evoke a feeling of wilderness. Here, mere yards from drivers sitting in climate-controlled cockpits and, very likely, gabbing on cellphones, is a place where you can see the blooms of water lilies in quiet ponds whose waters ripple only to the movement of a green frog or painted turtle. Or you can see swamp rose mallow blooming in the marsh. Or you can become lost and mired in the muck. It's that wild.

Woodlands Red maple, which prospers in wet conditions, dominates the woodlands of Montezuma. The red maple's fruits are in winged pairs, usually at less than 90 degrees to one another. You may recall finding these as a child and tossing them in the air, where they spun gently earthward like a helicopter coming in for a landing. Leaves are silver below but darkish green above, with saw-toothed lobes. Also present are white oaks, ash, and eastern cottonwood. The forest floor can be a wonder of wildflowers—yellow iris, mayapples, and mustards among them—in the spring and summer.

Grasslands The refuge maintains small amounts of grassland, critical to many songbirds and some species of ducks, such as mallards. Here grow warm-season grasses, such as the bluestems and switchgrasses. During summer, the bright yellow petals of black-eyed Susans liberally dot these fields.

■ **ANIMAL LIFE** Like so many other refuges in the mid-Atlantic, this is a place where people come in search of birds. A careful eye, however, will reveal other creatures, such as a red fox dancing through the snow of midwinter.

Birds Since the refuge was founded, almost 250 species of birds have been spotted at Montezuma. Warblers teem in spring. Fall and spring bring the legions of waterfowl: more than 80,000 Canada geese, 12,000 snow geese, 1,000,000 mallards, and 25,000 black ducks—more when the leaves turn than when they bud.

Killdeer

Montezuma's claim to fame is the bald eagle. These birds, once on extinction's brink but now returning to areas from which they had vanished, breed in the refuge (see sidebar, Blackwater Refuge, p. 40). The return of the eagle, like the restoration of the marshes, results from humans reversing the harm they have done to the environment. Assaulted by destruction of habitat and pesticides, bald eagles declined. Conservationists, private and public, fought to bring them back. In 1976, captive-reared eaglets were released at Montezuma, the first effort to do so in North America. It worked: Bald eagles were recently removed from the endangered-species list.

Although almost 300 miles from the seacoast and its Atlantic Flyway, Montezuma hosts hordes of shorebirds, heading north in the spring. Killdeer and yellowlegs scurry across the mudflats. Look carefully, and you may see dowitchers scrounging along water's edge.

Mammals White-tailed deer abound in the refuge. Fox are prominent residents, although they are shy and not easily seen. The red fox is more visible than the gray fox; 1 in 20 visitors to the refuge reports sighting them in the early morning or evening. Hidden away are the moles, voles, and the deer mice, which hide in fallen leaves and grasses. Of course, as with any marshland, muskrat are present, using their vertically flattened tails like oars to propel them through the water.

Reptiles and amphibians Bullfrogs, green frogs, snapping turtles, and painted turtles are the reptiles and amphibians that visitors are most likely to see in Montezuma's pools, impoundments, and ponds. Look along the shorelines, amidst the greenery that serves these quiet creatures as camouflage.

Invertebrates You may not see them at all, but they are here. Whirligig beetles circle on the placid surface of a pond. The larvae of mayflies, as fierce in appearance and demeanor as in their adult stage, is fairylike. Look closely in Montezuma's many waters, where they thrive.

ACTIVITIES

■ **CAMPING:** No camping is allowed on the refuge; camping facilities are available 5 miles south of the refuge at Cayoga State Park, on Rte. 89.

■ **WILDLIFE OBSERVATION:** You're not likely to be alone at Montezuma, except midweek, off-season: Around 160,000 people visit the refuge annually. But it is a big place,

HUNTING AND FISHING During the fall, the refuge is open to **deer** hunting: archery, shotgun, and muzzle-loader. There is also a limited **waterfowl** hunt. Contact the refuge for specific dates for each season and for information on hunting permits.

Fishing is not allowed on Montezuma NWR; however, there are three public fishing sites on the barge canals that run alongside the refuge property. Though not a major attraction, the canal fishing offers warm-water species like **carp**, **panfish**, and **bullheads** and an occasional **largemouth bass**.

and people do spread out. Along the wildlife drive there are abundant opportunities to see birds and deer. Benning Marsh and May's Point Pool are good viewing spots for shorebirds, especially during autumn. Late winter, if you can stand the cold, is a good time to view waterfowl, because geese gather here until spring's warmth sends them north. Bear in mind that it can be quite chilly at this time. Easier weather comes in August and September, when shorebirds and wading birds gather. The hot spot of birding at this refuge is probably the observation tower at Tschache Pool, where eagles may be seen with some certainty. Bring your binoculars.

■ **PHOTOGRAPHY:** The birds at Montezuma are favorite photo subjects. The best time to capture waterfowl is November, when the refuge is packed with migratory birds. Bring along a long lens for a close-up shot of a bald eagle from the observation tower at Tschache Pool.

■ **HIKES AND WALKS:** Two-mile-long Esker Brook Trail is the refuge's walking path. It is actually links three trails: Ridge, Brook, and Orchard. Open January to October. Stay on the designated pathway. There is no bushwhacking off the trail in the rest of the refuge.

■ **CROSS-COUNTRY SKIING:** Skiing is permitted, but check with refuge headquarters on where and when. Options vary with the weather.

■ **SEASONAL EVENTS:** The biggest draws at the refuge are the spring and fall migrations. The refuge celebrates National Wildlife Refuge Week in October with special events.

■ **PUBLICATIONS:** Refuge brochures on birds, wildflowers, and plants.

Wertheim NWR
Shirley, New York

Carmans River, Wertheim NWR

Flowing into the sea at Shirley, on the south shore of Long Island, is the Carmans River, a substantial stream—and a wild one by Long Island standards. The stream and its environs are fine enough to have been designated one of the state's Natural and Scenic rivers. As it nears the ocean and gathers the waters of tributaries, the Carmans bisects Wertheim NWR, one of the last undeveloped estuary systems on Long Island.

Because Wertheim refuge protects vestiges of natural treasures that Long Island once had in abundance, it does not offer an extensive array of activities for visitors. But what *is* there is well worth seeing. Here is Long Island as Walt Whitman might have known it, as he wandered old Paumanock's sandy shores, dreaming his poems, so rich with images of land, sky, and water.

HISTORY

Cecile and Maurice Wertheim, who had maintained the area as a private waterfowl hunting preserve, gave the refuge to the U.S. Fish & Wildlife Service in 1947. Another parcel was donated in 1974. It now totals 2,600 acres. Wertheim refuge is headquarters for the Long Island NWR Complex, nine refuges, most off-limits to the public and established primarily to protect imperiled species of plants and animals. Besides Wertheim, two other refuges in the complex are generally accessible: Morton and Target Rock. Another property, Oyster Bay refuge, can be accessed by boaters from Long Island Sound.

GETTING THERE

From Route 27A (Montauk Highway), turn south onto Smith Rd., just east of the Carmans River. Go 0.33 mi. to the refuge entrance on the right.

■ **SEASON:** Refuge open year-round Mon.–Sat.

- **HOURS:** General refuge: 7:30 a.m.–4 p.m.. Headquarters: weekdays, 8 a.m.–4:30 p.m.
- **FEES:** None.
- **ADDRESS:** Long Island National Wildlife Refuge Complex, P.O. Box 21, Shirley, NY 11967
- **TELEPHONE:** 516/286-0485

TOURING WERTHEIM

- **BY AUTOMOBILE:** There is no auto touring at Long Island refuges.
- **BY FOOT:** White Oak Nature Trail begins near headquarters. It has 1.5-mile and 3-mile loops. Indian Landing Trail, through pine barrens, is accessible by boat and canoe from the Carmans River.
- **BY BICYCLE:** No bikes are allowed.
- **BY CANOE, KAYAK, OR BOAT:** There is a launch site just off the Montauk Hwy., just outside the refuge, that provides access to the Carmans River.

WHAT TO SEE

- **LANDSCAPE AND CLIMATE** Long Island is a glacial moraine, a series of ridges consisting mostly of gravel and rubble left by the last glacier. The Wertheim refuge in this complex lies on the outwash plain, south shore (Atlantic Ocean side) of Long Island, a level area where running water deposited glacial debris sloping toward the sea. The climate is influenced by the ocean. For New York, it is relatively moderate, with the ocean waters cooling the shore in the summer. Coastal storms in fall and winter can bring high surf, pounding rain, and occasional heavy, wet snow.

- **PLANT LIFE** Wertheim is today as most of coastal Long Island once was. Forests of conifers and hardwoods are less majestic than expansive, with tidal marshes seaward and freshwater wetlands inland.
Forests Pitch pine is naturally dominant. But when fire (a fairly frequent occurrence) or disease destroys the pines, the oaks take over. Their crowns shade pine seedlings, curbing their growth. Here are pine stands, oak stands, and, where the two are at war for territory, mixed forests of both.
Grasslands Refuge grasslands include the bluestem grasses, annual meadow grass, rye, and timothy.
Wetlands Salt marsh and brackish marsh are the most prominent features here. The dominant plants are salt-marsh cordgrass in the low marshes and salt-meadow cordgrass in places of slightly higher elevation, reached only by the higher tides.

- **ANIMAL LIFE**
Birds More than 300 species of

Pine warbler

birds can be found here. Pine warblers, naturally, haunt the pinewoods, feeding on seeds in the summer. Ospreys soar overhead. Inland is the largest breeding population of wood ducks on Long Island.

Mammals White-tailed deer rove out of the refuge to consume the shrubs of homeowners and crops of those farmers who remain. Red foxes, mink, weasel, shrew, and muskrats may also be seen by patient observers.

Reptiles and amphibians The occasional loggerhead sea turtle visits the shores of the refuge, but visitors rarely see them. Box turtles, on the other hand, are often easy to spot in ponds and along streams. Spring peepers, wood frogs, and gray tree frogs breed in seasonal ponds.

ACTIVITIES

■ **CAMPING:** Camping is not allowed on the refuge. Camping facilities are available at nearby Smithpoint Beach and South Haven Park.

■ **WILDLIFE OBSERVATION:** Boating the Carmans River provides a great opportunity to see wildlife. Otherwise, take White Oak or Indian Landing trails. White oaks can be rather large trees with broad crowns. Leaves are longish, narrow, and have rounded lobes. In autumn, white oak leaves turn orange and brown and tend to hang on late in the season. Telltale signs on the ground: acorns, lots of them, until the squirrels arrive.

■ **PHOTOGRAPHY:** Along White Oak Trail are an observation blind and observation platform.

HUNTING AND FISHING Fishing for stocked **trout** and **white perch** is permitted only from a boat—there is no fishing from the banks of the Carmans River. **Blue crabs** can also be caught in summer.

No hunting is allowed at Wertheim.

Erie NWR
Guys Mills, Pennsylvania

Canada geese, Erie NWR

Tucked into the rural countryside of northwestern Pennsylvania, Erie National Wildlife Refuge has a beauty both subtle and spectacular: meadows carpeted with the glorious gold of black-eyed Susans; the resplendent colors of the male wood duck, white speckles on its chestnut chest, green head, pink bill, and eyes of fiery red; the flower of the trout lily, bronze on the outside and a delicate yellow on the inside. Even during winter, color bursts through the monochromatic landscape— brilliant red berries of winterberry holly can be found among the ghostly gray forms of dormant deciduous trees and the snow-laden boughs of hemlocks.

Erie has two units: Sugar Lake, 5,200 acres and the site of the refuge headquarters and Visitor Center, and Seneca, 10 miles to the north, 3,600 acres in a labyrinth of swampy bottomlands, streams, and bogs. The small streams that lace Seneca are mainly tributaries of a waterway called French Creek. More a river than a creek, it is a marvel. French Creek's almost pristine waters contain biological diversity that few other streams in eastern North America can match.

HISTORY

In the middle of the 17th century, the Erie Native American peoples were embroiled in a feud with the Iroquois, their neighbors to the east. Although the Erie were able fighters, they were no match for their adversaries and were nearly exterminated. After the American Revolution, lands in the area were given to soldiers who fought in the Colonial Army. Typically, logging and draining projects turned virgin land into farmland. Forests and wetlands disappeared. Trapping of beaver and, later, destruction of their habitat further altered the environment. That's because the dams that beavers build help create wetlands. Without the dams, wetlands fill up and become field or forest.

With the passage of time, logging became unproductive (although hemlock bark was much prized for tanning), and farming in the region declined. Many farmers became part-timers who depended on other work to earn their living. This corner of Pennsylvania remained fairly removed from the onslaught of environmental destruction that swept over nearby areas. One of the reasons why French Creek—so named by George Washington—is productive is that its waters have largely escaped the effects of agriculture and urban development. In 1959, Erie NWR was established to conserve wetland habitat for waterfowl that were dwindling in numbers elsewhere. Today, the refuge serves the needs of many other species besides waterfowl, including the beaver. Some 50,000 people visit Erie NWR each year.

GETTING THERE

From US 79, take Exit 36 to Meadville. Continue 7 mi. on PA 27. Shortly after passing a furniture store on the right, take PA 3032 for 3 mi. into Guys Mills. At a four-way stop, take PA 198 for 0.8 mi. Just after passing a cemetery on the left, the entrance road to the refuge (Wood Duck Lane) will be on the right.

■ **SEASON:** Refuge open year-round.

■ **HOURS:** General refuge: Open daily, half-hour before sunrise to sunset, unless posted otherwise. Headquarters, including Visitor Center: weekdays, 8 a.m.–4:30 p.m. Depending on availability of assistance by interns, headquarters may be open some weekends during the summer.

■ **FEES:** None.

■ **ADDRESS:** 11296 Wood Duck Lane, Guys Mills, PA 16327

■ **TELEPHONE:** 814/789-3585

TOURING ERIE

■ **BY AUTOMOBILE:** There is no designated auto drive. However, local roads through and near the refuge can put you in touch with deer, wild turkeys, and songbirds.

■ **BY FOOT:** Erie has four trails, three in Sugar Lake and one in Seneca. The

Northern cardinal

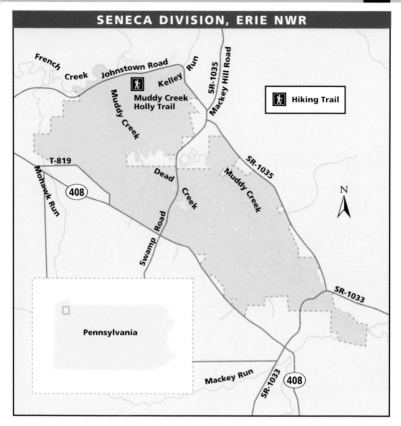

SENECA DIVISION, ERIE NWR

trails in the refuge are designed so that trekkers can see virtually all major habitats. Some have sections covered with wood chips for easy going. Many stretches of trail are bordered by wildflowers, in season.

WHAT TO SEE

■ **LANDSCAPE AND CLIMATE** Here is where the last Ice Age glaciers finally ground to a halt. Some of the river valleys in this region, part of the Allegheny Plateau, were gouged by ice. Rubble dropped by the retreating ice accumulated, from 5 feet to 100 feet deep, over sandstone and shale, up to 400 feet deep, that dates back some 400 million years, the results of sedimentation during a time when ancient seas covered the land. The result of this geological give-and-take is a land of rolling hills with valleys in between—rugged but by no means dishpan flat.

The Erie refuge lies within the Allegheny Plateau, but by virtue of its draining is part of the Ohio River ecosystem, at least the way scientists categorize such things. French Creek starts in the very southwestern tip of New York, flows through northwestern Pennsylvania into the Allegheny River, which empties into the Ohio. The Ohio's waters eventually meet the Mississippi. And so the waters of Erie flow into the sea.

Cold in the winter, moderately warm in summer: That has been the climactic history of Erie. Midwinter temperatures are often just above or below freezing. Lake-effect snow off Lake Erie often blankets the refuge, making

SUGAR LAKE DIVISION, ERIE NWR

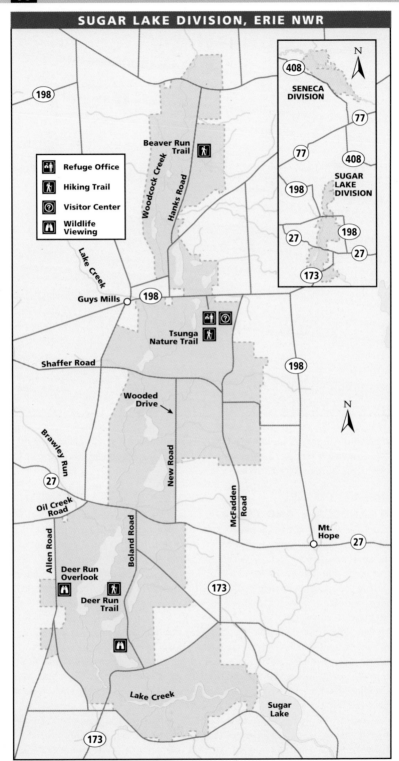

198

408

SENECA DIVISION

77

77

408

SUGAR LAKE DIVISION

198

198

27

198

27

173

Beaver Run Trail

Woodcock Creek

Hanks Road

Refuge Office

Hiking Trail

Visitor Center

Wildlife Viewing

Lake Creek

Guys Mills   198

Tsunga Nature Trail

Shaffer Road

198

Wooded Drive

Brawley Run

27

Oil Creek Road

Allen Road

Boland Road

New Road

McFadden Road

Mt. Hope   27

Deer Run Overlook

Deer Run Trail

173

Lake Creek

Sugar Lake

173

N

N

cross-country skiing popular here. Temperatures at the height of summer are generally in the eighties.

■ **PLANT LIFE** A wide diversity of plant communities within a relatively small area makes Erie an especially interesting spot from an ecological standpoint. Here is a microcosm of what the region was like when the Erie Indians were its only human occupants.

Forests Erie's towering hemlocks, in groves like natural cathedrals, make for a cool, dark, hushed, and damp forest. Hemlocks integrate with deciduous trees in many areas. There are beech, tulips, yellow birch, basswood, and, on higher ground, a scattering of sugar maple, which help make autumns here blaze with color. The forest floor is dotted with such wildflowers as trout lilies, violets, marsh marigolds, and spring beauties.

Grasslands Although forest wildflowers largely bloom in spring, many meadow species put on a show from summer into fall. The grassland areas of the refuge are colored by black-eyed Susans, milkweed, Queen Anne's lace, blue-eyed grass, and butter-and-eggs. Warm-season native grasses, such as switch grass, big bluestem, little bluestem and Indian grass, have been planted in fields to provide cover for mallards and blue-winged teal nesting in upland meadows. The grasses grow in tall bunches that help conceal eggs and nestlings from predators, especially crows.

Wetlands At least half of Erie consists of wetlands. Many of them are managed, some by refuge staff, some by beavers. Look for cattails and water lilies, perhaps cardinal flowers on the edges. Erie has unusual wetlands called shrub fens (see sidebar p. 99), where a sharp eye may spot some very rare plants, including thin-leaved cotton grass and drooping bluegrass.

Great blue heron, fishing

■ **ANIMAL LIFE** Some National Wildlife Refuges in the mid-Atlantic region are famed for immense assemblages of certain animal species, such as the snow geese that annually visit refuges along the Delaware Bay. Erie does not have such spectacular masses of animals. What it does have is a remarkably large *number* of species, some quite abundant, and many of which can be seen with relative ease.

Birds About 237 species of birds have been regularly seen at Erie, and several

Saw-whet owl

others have visited on occasion. The environmental good health of the refuge is evident in the fact that 112 of these bird species also breed here. These include bald eagles, eastern bluebirds, tree swallows, pileated woodpeckers, great blue herons, green herons, mallards, hooded mergansers and wood ducks. The latter are a feature in Erie's swamps, where you will find a major breeding population of this gorgeous species. Several hundred young wood ducks are produced each year.

When spring arrives at Erie, so do warblers. The woods can seem to be alive with them. Among the species: yellow warbler, green-throated warbler, and yellowthroat. Erie also hosts several species that most any birder would be proud to have on a life list: American bittern, Henslow's sparrow, black tern, upland sandpiper, and the saw-whet owl.

The saw-whet owl is charming. Only 8 inches long, with a head that seems too large for its small body, it sometimes appears so tame that it allows people to approach within a few feet as it roosts in conifers. The saw-whet is generally a creature of boreal forests, but it heads south to places such as Erie in the winter. Its name comes from its call, which sounds like a mill saw being sharpened.

Mammals If you are lucky, you may see a mink hunting along the water's edge or a black bear shuffling through the woods. Mammals that are easier to see are white-tailed deer, red fox, red squirrels, fox and gray squirrels, muskrats, cottontail rabbits, and woodchucks. Beaver, as noted, now abound at Erie. Some live in dome-shaped lodges engineered of sticks and mud. Others make their homes in burrows, dug into banks.

Reptiles and amphibians Reptiles and, to an even greater degree, amphibians are often creatures of hidden places. Not many visitors here will ever see the retiring eastern smooth green snake. Green as grass—a foot and a half long—and known as the grass snake, it hunts meadows for spiders and insects. Nor are the elfin northern dusky salamander and red-backed salamander easily visible. They hide under fallen logs and rock and in leaf litter.

But some of Erie's reptiles and amphibians are not so shy. Painted turtles bask on logs and rocks, soaking up the sun. Snapping turtles float at the water's surface or wander across trails. Bullfrogs and green frogs announce their presence in the water with their calls and often float for anyone with a questing eye to observe.

Fish French Creek is a paradise for fish. As far as is known, the stream has not lost any native fish. More than 80 species inhabit its waters. Prominent among them are darters, finger-length little creatures that zip about the bottom. They seldom rise higher because they lack a swim bladder, the internal gas bag that acts like a float enabling the majority of fish to achieve buoyancy in the water. Darters in general are threatened by siltation of the streams in which they live. This is not a problem in French Creek. Also inhabiting the waters of Erie are trout, sunfish, and largemouth bass.

Invertebrates At Erie you can find some invertebrates that are rare elsewhere.

The Harris checkerspot butterfly adds to the beauty of summer days. The bottom of French Creek provides a home for freshwater mussels, including the endangered rifleshell and clubshell. The clubshell, in particular, is in a dire strait. Its historic range in the United States is only 5 percent of what it once was.

Woodchuck

ACTIVITIES

■ **WILDLIFE OBSERVA-TION:** Not surprisingly, Beaver Run Trail is a good place to spot beavers, especially toward the end of the day. So is Tsuga Trail, which has a boardwalk over a beaver pond. The woods around Deer Run Trail are the home of the crow-size pileated woodpecker. You may see these birds, with their flaming red crest; if not, you may hear their jackhammer banging on trees or see chips of wood on the ground, the leftovers of their work. Most of the impoundments afford views of waterfowl. Mergansers and mallards are easier to see than wood ducks, which are ultracautious. If you do not see them on the

---

THE MYSTERIOUS FEN *Fen* is a word that speaks of dank, mysterious places, where Celtic rebels in Scotland and Ireland found safe haven against the armies of the English Crown. It is a place where banshees prowl and fairies cavort. Fens are places where one can literally walk on water. The water, however, is largely underground, held there by soils that resist drainage. But there are pools in places where water seeps to the surface. It makes the going soggy and squishy, unfit for a jaunt on even a bright summer's day. And bright days in the foggy fens are few and far between.

Fens are not common worldwide. A handful of them, some only a few acres, are scattered about Erie NWR's inner recesses. Here, shrubby vegetation grows on islets of high ground amid the morass. Plants such as the slender spikerush and swamp-fly honeysuckle, seldom seen elsewhere, are present here at Erie, well preserved.

HUNTING AND FISHING There is abundant hunting on the refuge. **White-tailed deer** hunts take place in Oct. and Jan. There are two **wild turkey** seasons, (one in the spring and one in the fall), and other **upland game** hunting is permitted during various seasons throughout the year.

There is an abundance of fishing opportunities present on the refuge. You may fish along the banks of a number of the refuge waters and may use nonmotorized boats on Pool 9 only. Anglers most often find **panfish**, **perch**, **bass**, and, in late spring, the occasional **trout**. Before hunting or fishing on the refuge, obtain a leaflet from the Visitor Center.

water, check the overhanging trees. Unlike most ducks, "woodies," as hunters call them, often perch.

■ **PHOTOGRAPHY:** The refuge has one photographic blind. It is rigged with interior slats and openings on which to rest binoculars or a camera to take photographs. The blind is popular for photographs of deer and waterfowl.

■ **HIKES AND WALKS:** Muddy Creek Holly Trail, in Seneca, is more rustic than the other trails. It has a boardwalk so that hikers can negotiate wetlands easily and in safe fashion. Veterans of the area warn newcomers not to wander off the trail because, in the words of an Erie refuge official, this is "forest primeval." It is easy to become lost and even mired in dangerous mud. The trail's name comes from the valley of Muddy Creek, a tributary of French Creek, and from the profuse growths of winterberry holly that grow on its margins.

The most popular trail is Tsuga, named after the scientific genus of the eastern hemlock, which grows in this area. Accessible near headquarters, this is a 1.2-mile or 1.6-mile loop, depending on whether you take an offshoot. A boardwalk passes over a beaver pond. Beaver Run Trail is a 1-mile loop with a short spur that also goes by beaver habitat.

Deer Run Trail is another loop of 3 miles, skirting ponds and passing through mixed hardwood and hemlock forests and meadows that are speckled with black-eyed Susans in the summer.

Trails in the refuge are also open for cross-country skiing and snowshoeing. Typically, there is sufficient snow on the ground throughout the winter to make both activities possible.

■ **PUBLICATIONS:** Refuge pamphlets describing trails, plants, and wildlife.

John Heinz NWR at Tinicum
Philadelphia, Pennsylvania

Urban wetland against Philadelphia skyline, John Heinz NWR

There are wild and woolly places in Pennsylvania, where black bears raiding backyard trash cans do not make news, where white-tailed deer are an everyday sight, and where the woods thunder to the wingbeats of male ruffed grouse, performing their courting dance. Ironically, the largest freshwater tidal marsh in Pennsylvania, one of the few places in the Quaker State where imperiled red-bellied turtles and southern leopard frogs can be found, is not in the boondocks but in the city of Philadelphia. John Heinz NWR at Tinicum is like a trip to the backcountry within city limits. Here, even at the margins of the Philadelphia International Airport, a few miles from the heart of town, more than 100,000 people each year—many of them schoolchildren from the city—come out to enjoy a respite from urban stresses, amidst wildlife in a place of marshlands and tidal streams.

HISTORY

Tinicum Marsh, the heart of Heinz refuge, was once almost 6,000 acres. Dredging, diking, and other human activities reduced it to a mere 200 acres by the 1950s. In 1955, Gulf Oil Company donated a tract of 145 acres to the city of Philadelphia, creating the Tinicum Wildlife Preserve. Of today's 1,200-acre NWR, 250 acres remain tidal marsh while the rest are impoundments, uplands, and fields. John Heinz NWR was congressionally established in 1972 after local citizens fought against turning the area into highways and a landfill. The late Pennsylvania senator John Heinz supported the effort to make the site a National Wildlife Refuge, and today it provides fine environmental education programs for area residents and their children. The U.S. Fish & Wildlife Service is the federal agency that provides stewardship of the most urbanized refuge in the NWR System. A $5 million environmental education center should be completed in the summer of 2000.

GETTING THERE

From northbound US 95, take PA 291 at the Airport Exit. At the light, turn right on Bartram Ave. At the first light, go left on 84th St. At the second light, go left on Lindberg Blvd. The refuge entrance and Visitor Contact Station are two blocks farther, on the right.

■ **SEASON:** Refuge open year-round.

■ **HOURS:** Refuge open 8 a.m.–sunset; Visitor Contact Station open 9 a.m.–4 p.m., daily. Refuge headquarters open 8 a.m.–4 p.m., weekdays .

■ **FEES:** None.

■ **ADDRESS:** John Heinz NWR at Tinicum, 2 International Plaza, Ste. 104, Philadelphia, PA 19113

■ **TELEPHONE:** Visitor Contact Station: 215/365-3118. Refuge headquarters: 610/521-0662 (Note: Number may change in 2000.)

TOURING HEINZ

■ **BY AUTOMOBILE:** There is no wildlife drive on the refuge.

■ **BY FOOT:** Heinz refuge offers 10 miles of trails.

■ **BY BICYCLE:** Gravel trails are open to biking, but at your own risk.

■ **BY CANOE, KAYAK, OR BOAT:** Behind the Visitor Contact Station is a ramp where small, nonmotorized boats can be launched on Darby Creek, which leads into the Delaware River. This is an excellent place to see wildlife. Warning: Boats can become mired at low tide.

WHAT TO SEE

■ **LANDSCAPE AND CLIMATE** The refuge lies in the Atlantic Coastal Plain at its margin with the Piedmont, its geology obscured by urbanization surrounding it. Here are marshlands, upland woods, thickets, and fields around the edges of impoundments. Almost all of the refuge has been altered by human activities, some in yesteryear for the bad, today altered again to restore nature. The heart of the refuge is Tinicum Marsh, along Darby Creek, upstream from

Canada geese

where it flows into the Delaware River, influenced by the tides, although far from the sea.

■ PLANT LIFE

Marsh Spatterdock and duckweed coat the water's surface. There are no cordgrasses here. Although the marsh feels the pulse of the tides, the water this far from the sea is fresh. Cordgrasses, typical of salt marshes, are adapted to saline waters. Cattails, which are freshwater plants, are common. Wild rice, once a dominant plant and a precious food for waterfowl, is almost gone.

Fields The fields at Heinz refuge are far from "virgin," with many plants that normally inhabit ecologically disturbed areas: milkweed, ragweed, and aster all abound. Nonetheless, these fields provide valuable food and cover for a host of creatures. Here are bees and butterflies aplenty.

> **HUNTING AND FISHING** The refuge offers an annual organized fishing program especially for youngsters and general fishing for the public. Species include **largemouth bass** and **panfish**. Some of the biggest **northern pike** caught in Pennsylvania have been hooked in the waters of this area.
>
> There is no hunting at the Heinz refuge.

■ ANIMAL LIFE

Some creatures, such as muskrats and raccoons, northern water snakes, and great blue herons, can be seen here year-round. Multitudes of others, like tree swallows and the willow flycatcher, visit seasonally.

Birds Migrant birds, using the Atlantic Coastal Flyway, find Heinz refuge a good place to stop, rest, and feed. More than 280 species have been seen here. Look for great blue herons, egrets, Canada geese, and some shorebirds, especially killdeer.

Mammals White-tailed deer and muskrats are the mammals visitors are most likely to see. Muskrats, somewhat smaller than a house cat, are aquatic rodents. They build lodges of reeds, sedges, and other aquatic vegetation in the shallows. Unlike beavers, which swim with downward thrusts of their laterally flattened tails, muskrats propel themselves through the water by sculling, with tails that are flattened vertically, like oars.

ACTIVITIES

■ **WILDLIFE OBSERVATION:** In 1999 a new Visitor Center was in construction, to open in a year or so. Brush and woods along the trails are good spots to see warblers. Spring and fall are times to watch marshes and impoundments for waterfowl. There is an observation platform, two levels high, over an impoundment less than a mile from the Visitor Contact Station. Three blinds, for observation and photography, are located on the trails.

■ **HIKES AND WALKS:** A 10-mile trail loop, with offshoots, starts at the Visitor Contact Station. Boardwalks into marshes extend off the loop. The best one is near the Visitor Contact Station. A trail of about 3.3 miles around the East Impoundment is a favorite walking area.

■ **PUBLICATIONS:** Refuge pamphlets available at Visitor Contact Station.

Back Bay NWR
Virginia Beach, Virginia

Dike road and bay, Back Bay NWR

At dawn, tracks in the sand of a barrier beach bespeak a reproductive ritual root-ed in the Mesozoic era, the Age of Reptiles. A swath of sand a yard or more wide has been roiled into a path leading from the sea to the upper beach. Another path leads back to the water and disappears in the wave wash. During the night a female loggerhead turtle, a massive sea creature weighing hundreds of pounds, has come to the shores of Back Bay NWR to lay her eggs in the sand. The logger-head is an endangered species, and the chief reason for its decline is that beaches where it can nest undisturbed have become rare. The beaches of this refuge, which lies on a barrier island peninsula, not only work to protect Back Bay from the Atlantic surf but they also serve as the northern margins of the loggerhead's breeding grounds.

The refuge, south of Virginia Beach, is centered on a barrier that fronts Back Bay and, to the south, meets North Carolina's Currituck Sound, whose waters feed the bay. The refuge also includes marshy islands in the bay and parcels scattered on the mainland (not yet open to public) as well as open bay water. Back Bay is a classic mid-Atlantic estuarine area, with marshes, fresh and brackish, as well as low woodlands, stunted and gnarled by the sea wind.

HISTORY

Back Bay was legendary waterfowling area from the middle of the 1800s to the early 20th century. Hunting clubs, owned mostly by the wealthy, proliferated here on lands and marshes farmed by settlers since early Colonial days. The refuge was founded in 1938, one of the earliest National Wildlife Refuges established to pro-vide habitat for migrating and wintering waterfowl. It now consists of almost 8,000 acres, and it draws a substantial crowd of visitors over the course of the year, nearly 125,000 people.

GETTING THERE

From Norfolk, take US 64 to VA Rte. 44 to Virginia Beach. Exit on Birdneck Rd., travel 3 to 4 mi., and then go right on General Booth Blvd. for 2 to 3 mi. Turn left onto Princess Anne Rd. Go left again at the first stoplight at Sandbridge Rd. for 3 mi. At Sandpiper Rd., go right and head south for 4 mi. to the refuge entrance.

■ **SEASON:** General refuge open year-round, sunrise to sunset.

■ **HOURS:** The office is open Mon.–Sat., 8 a.m.–4 p.m.; Sun., 9 a.m.–4 p.m.

■ **FEES:** $2 per person, foot or bike. Private vehicles: $5 for whole car. School groups and children under 16 are free.

■ **ADDRESS:** Back Bay NWR, 4005 Sandpiper Rd., Virginia Beach, VA 23456

■ **TELEPHONE:** 757/721-2412

TOURING BACK BAY

■ **BY AUTOMOBILE:** There is no auto-tour route here. However, the Back Bay Relocation Foundation runs an electric tram from Little Island City Park, adjoining the refuge.

■ **BY FOOT:** There are more than 7 miles of trails along the barrier, atop dikes and on boardwalks. Some are closed seasonally to protect nesting birds.

■ **BY BICYCLE:** Dike Trail is open to bikes during appropriate seasons.

■ **BY CANOE, KAYAK, OR BOAT:** Next to refuge headquarters is a launch for car-top (nonmotorized) boats. Trailers are not permitted.

WHAT TO SEE

Black-crowned night-heron

■ **LANDSCAPE AND CLIMATE** The glaciers of the last Ice Age stopped at New York's Long Island, far to the north of Back Bay. However, they helped shape this estuary—or, rather, their retreat did. As the glaciers melted, the sea level rose. When the glaciers held sway, Back Bay was dry land.

As the sea rose, however, it filled with water. Currents and waves, which have shaped barriers by depositing sand all along the mid-Atlantic coast, created the barrier beach island that shields Back Bay from the force of the ocean. The refuge lies at the northern tip of the barrier and the bay.

On the sea side of the barrier, surf roars against the shore. On the landward,

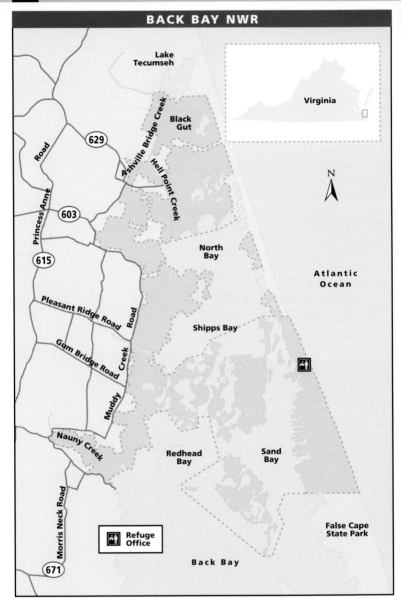

BACK BAY NWR

Lake
Tecumseh

Black
Gut

Ashville Bridge Creek

Hell Point Creek

629

603

615

Princess Anne

Road

Virginia

N

North
Bay

Atlantic
Ocean

Pleasant Ridge Road

Road

Gum Bridge Road

Creek

Shipps Bay

Muddy

Creek

Nauny Creek

Redhead
Bay

Sand
Bay

Morris Neck Road

Refuge
Office

False Cape
State Park

671

Back Bay

western side, estuarine waters are generally tranquil and provide a rich soup of
nutrients that feeds plant and animal life. The climate is chilly but seldom cold in
winter, hot as blazes in summer—temperatures often above 90 degrees—except
when the sea breeze takes hold, and it is most amenable in spring and fall.

■ **PLANT LIFE** The plant communities of Back Bay are highly manipulated by
humans as well as influenced by nature. Plant life ranges from hardy sea oats on
the barrier beach dunes to freshwater marshes on the barrier, impounded by
wildlife managers.
Dunes Here, sea oats, tall and graceful, fight to hold the sand against relentless

wind and waves. Their horizontally spreading underground roots anchor the sand against forces that would otherwise sweep it away.

Maritime forest Behind the dunes, on uplands, are wind-whipped forests, largely of loblolly pine and scrubby live oaks, stunted by the sea but, nevertheless, providing cover for wildlife such as deer and marsh rabbits.

Shrublands Wax myrtle, highbush blueberry, bayberry, wild black cherry, and persimmon form shrub communities in some upland areas.

Marshes Adjacent to the sea (right beyond the dunes) but protected from it by the barrier, the marshes of Back Bay support plants that thrive in fresh and brackish waters: three-square bulrush, spikerushes, and smartweed.

■ **ANIMAL LIFE** Coastal barrier islands squeeze a large variety of plant communities into an extremely narrow strip. The Back Bay barrier, for instance, is only about a mile wide. The compression creates a great diversity of habitats and many subtle interfaces between them, favoring many types of wildlife.

Birds More than 300 species of birds—about half the total number seen in the lower 48 states—can be seen here. Endangered piping plovers skitter on beaches during the breeding season. Bald eagles soar overhead. During the winter, 10,000 or so snow geese visit. Many shorebirds, such as greater yellowlegs and ruddy turnstones, are abundant in spring. Be sure to use the refuge's bird list when you visit Back Bay.

Mammals There is a good chance that you will see white-tailed deer on the refuge. Keep a patient eye on the marshes to catch a glimpse of otters. These are river otters (sea otters live off the West Coast), which grow to about 4 feet in length and are brown on top, with a silver shine to their bellies. Equipped with webbed feet, they spend the day diving and fishing in the water. Their worn slides on banks of mud (or snow) can be a tipoff that you're looking in the right territory.

The smaller relative of the otter, the mink, lives here, too. But spotting one at Back Bay—or almost anyplace else—is a matter of chance. Muskrats, however, are far more common. Gray foxes roam at Back Bay and, unlike their red fox counterparts, they are sometimes active by day. Check the edge areas, where field and trees meet and where foxes like to hunt. Marsh rabbits are also abundant.

River otter

Reptiles and amphibians Living emeralds—green tree frogs—call from hidden places in brush and branches. Green frogs puddle in the ponds. Reptiles on this refuge include red-bellied, painted, eastern mud, and snapping turtles.

Black rat snakes and hognose snakes are abundant. So is the cottonmouth (aka water moccasin and a relative of the rattlesnake), one of the most venomous serpents in North America. Fully grown cottonmouths can be 6 feet long and as big around as a man's arm. They take their name from the whiteness of their lips and mouth, not from the softness of their bite.

Cottonmouths are aquatic, favoring the swamps, feeding largely on fish and frogs, even on infant alligators. They also lurk in high grass. At a glance, they closely resemble the nonvenomous northern water snake. Water snakes usually flee humans, unless they are cornered. Cottonmouths sometimes will not give an inch. If you see a feisty, brownish snake in or around water, give ground. If it rears up and opens its mouth, revealing a white interior that cannot be mistaken, move away quickly.

ACTIVITIES

■ **CAMPING AND SWIMMING:** No camping or swimming is allowed on the refuge. A state park adjacent to Back Bay refuge offers camping facilities. Fine ocean swimming opportunities abound in Virginia Beach.

■ **WILDLIFE OBSERVATION:** It is rare for visitors to see the loggerhead turtles; they lay their eggs at night in areas that are off-limits to the public. However, the refuge managers do allow people to view the hatching in specific places and times. Anyone interested should call the refuge ahead to arrange a time. Eggs are laid in late

OLDER THAN THE DINOSAURS Turtles are venerable creatures. They evolved before the world ever knew a dinosaur.

Jurassic Park notwithstanding, the dinosaurs are gone, but turtles remain. They are surprisingly adaptable. Box turtles and wood turtles spend most of their lives on land. Snapping turtles lurk in the water, surviving even pollution. The grandest turtles of them all live in the sea.

One of these is the loggerhead, a creature that can weigh 900 pounds but is generally only a third of that bulk. The female loggerhead comes ashore on sandy beaches from the Back Bay area south to nest during the summer. She emerges from the surf at night, materializing from the wave wash with an astounding suddenness. One minute the beach is empty. The next, a hulking form, with a massive head and a shell rough as weathered stone, lurches out of the sea, water running off her sides.

Slowly but with ultimate purpose, the turtle crawls up the beach; its legs are flippers that can power it through the ocean but are somewhat clumsy on land. When the turtle reaches sand high enough on the beach to thwart all but the most powerful tidal surge, she uses her hind flippers to dig a shallow depression (nest cavity) in the sand. She positions herself over the cavity, letting one egg drop from her body at a time; she will lay up a hundred eggs this way. Once finished, she covers the nest with sand. Unless unearthed by raccoons or other predators or roiled by storm waves, the young turtles will hatch in about two months, warmed by sun beating on the beach. Digging out of the sand, eyes fixed with determination on the seaward horizon, they skitter down the sloping beach toward the waves and disappear, as silently as their mother emerged to bring them into the world.

Volunteers may sign up to assist with the turtle hatches, which occur in late summer, generally August and early September. Contact the refuge for details.

Loggerhead turtle laying eggs

May, and the hatchings occur in mid-August.

The beach here offers wonderful opportunities to see waterbirds. In the area of the wetlands impoundments, wildlife sightings include songbirds, waterfowl, hawks, and owls. The Visitor Contact Station has several wildlife exhibits

■ HIKES AND WALKS:

Trails bring you close to the wild creatures that inhabit barrier islands. Boardwalk trails bring you close to the seabirds and marine life that live along the sea's edge. Seaside Trial and Dune Trail are short boardwalks into the beach, where sand and dune plants can be seen. Bay Trail, less than half a mile long,

HUNTING AND FISHING During the first week of Oct. there are hunts for **white-tailed deer** and **feral hogs**.

Freshwater fishing in certain impoundments is largely for **largemouth bass** and **panfish**. Casting from the ocean beaches can produce **striped bass** and **bluefish**.

reaches into the lagoons and marshes behind the barrier. The majority of trails skirt the impoundments and also bring walkers within view of the marshes on the bay side of the refuge.

■ SEASONAL EVENTS: October: National Wildlife Refuge Week.

■ PUBLICATIONS: Refuge brochures and books are available at the Visitor Contact Station.

Chincoteague NWR
Chincoteague, Virginia

Pony roundup, Chincoteague NWR

There are two Chincoteagues.

One is the wild, solitary Chincoteague, moving to the eternal rhythms of tide and wind, the pulses of migration, the cycles of the seasons. It is the Chincoteague of empty beaches on a mild March day, of ghost-gray sanderlings leaving their tracks behind each retreating wave, of hot, humid summer afternoons in a labyrinth of tidal creeks, where clapper rails click like pebbles smacked together and an otter splits the reflection of green cordgrass with its nose.

The other is a place that draws more than half a million summer vacationers, creating occasional traffic jams, all seeking sun and fun. And finding it, both on the beach and on nature trails.

HISTORY

Chincoteague is one of America's most popular national wildlife refuges. It occupies Virginia's half of the 37-mile-long island known as Assateague—named from the Indian word for "a muddy place"—that is part of the barrier chain protecting the Maryland and Virginia coast. (Confusingly, the majority of the refuge is *not* located on the neighboring island of Chincoteague—only about 400 acres are located there.) The refuge has also expanded to include all or parts of three smaller barrier islands. Much of the rest of the island is managed as a National Seashore by the National Park Service, while a portion of the Maryland side functions as Assateague State Park. Chincoteague NWR was established in 1943 and has grown over the years to just over 14,000 acres.

GETTING THERE

From the north, take Rte. 13 south from Pocomoke City for 10 mi.; from Virginia Beach, cross the Chesapeake Bay Bridge-Tunnel and head north on Rte. 13 for about 64 mi. At the junction with Rte. 175, turn east for 10 mi. to the town of

Chincoteague, left on Main St. for 0.4 mi., then right on Maddux Ave. Drive another 2.2 mi. across the Assateague Channel and onto Assateague Island.

■ **SEASON:** Refuge open year-round.

■ **HOURS:** General refuge: May–Sept., 5 a.m.–10 p.m.; April and Oct., 6 a.m.–8 p.m.; Nov.–March, 6 a.m.–6 p.m. Refuge Visitor Center open daily, 9 a.m.–4 p.m. Toms Cove Visitor Center (Assateague Island National Seashore) open daily, 9 a.m.–5 p.m. Hours subject to change annually.

■ **FEES:** Entrance fee $3 per car, $1 per hiker or biker, good for 7 days; free access with current Federal Duck Stamp. $12 annual pass also available.

■ **ADDRESS:** Chincoteague NWR, P.O. Box 62, Chincoteague, VA 23336

■ **TELEPHONE:** 757/336-6122

TOURING CHINCOTEAGUE

■ **BY AUTOMOBILE:** Cars are permitted on the main road leading to Toms Cove and for about a mile south, with oversand vehicles only (with proper permits) beyond that point. Toms Cove Hook is closed to all access during the nesting season, March 15 to August 31. Cars are also allowed on Wildlife Loop after 3 p.m. (see "Hikes and Walks").

■ **BY FOOT:** In addition to paved hiking/biking paths, 10 miles of wild beach, from the Toms Cove Visitor Center north to the Maryland line, are open to foot travel. Trails also lead from the far north side of Wildlife Loop to Wash Flats, a rarely visited area nearly 7 miles from the developed portion of the refuge. Hikers should check on conditions with refuge staff before leaving and should carry adequate water. From August 31 to March 15, Toms Cove Hook is open to hiking and oversand vehicles. All hiking or climbing on the easily damaged dunes is forbidden.

■ **BY BICYCLE:** Bikes are permitted on all main refuge roads, the Woodland Trail, Wildlife Loop, and several smaller paths linking the loop to Beach Road on the south and the Toms Cove Visitor Center on the east.

■ **BY CANOE, KAYAK, OR BOAT:** Boating is allowed on the refuge's tidal creeks and in Toms Cove but not in refuge impoundments. Boat access to Toms Cove Hook is restricted during the March 15 to August 31 nesting season.

CROWDS OR SOLITUDE Although Chincoteague covers nearly 17 miles of barrier island, most visitors hit only Toms Cove, the Wildlife Loop, and the swimming beach, all clustered near the south end.

Even on summer weekends, when traffic heading for the beach can clog the main road all the way back to the causeway, it is possible to find solitude by heading to the backcountry: the far reaches of the northern beach, the service road adjacent to the Wash Flats, or the canoe-accessible tidal creeks along Chincoteague Bay.

The worst crowds of the year come with the big summer holidays (Memorial Day, 4th of July, Labor Day) and especially for the famous pony-swim and auction held the last week of July. Even in midweek during the summer holiday season, Chincoteague will be busy, but usually it's not overwhelming.

Chincoteague in early spring and late autumn is almost empty of people, and the climate is quite mild and the insects are largely absent. In midwinter the refuge, while cold and damp, has a powerful charm.

CHINCOTEAGUE NWR

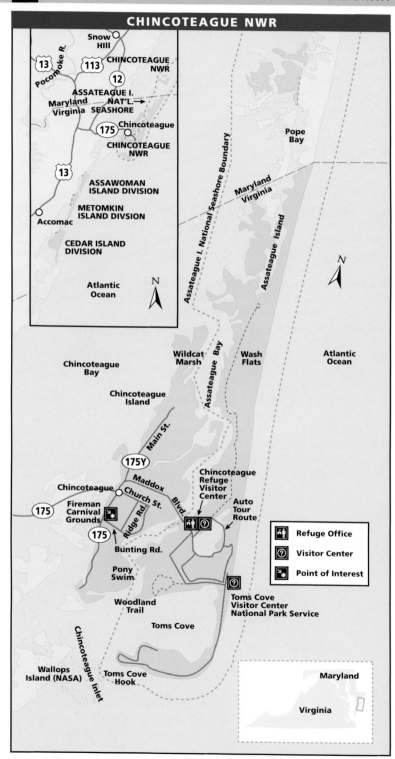

Snow Hill

13 113 CHINCOTEAGUE NWR

Pocomoke R.

12

ASSATEAGUE I. NAT'L. →
Maryland   SEASHORE
Virginia

175 Chincoteague

CHINCOTEAGUE NWR

13

ASSAWOMAN ISLAND DIVISION

METOMKIN ISLAND DIVSION

Accomac

CEDAR ISLAND DIVISION

Atlantic Ocean

N

Assateague I. National Seashore Boundary

Maryland
Virginia

Pope Bay

Assateague Island

N

Chincoteague Bay

Wildcat Marsh

Assateague Bay

Wash Flats

Atlantic Ocean

Chincoteague Island

Main St.

175Y

Maddox Blvd.

Chincoteague Church St.

175 Fireman Carnival Grounds

Ridge Rd.

Chincoteague Refuge Visitor Center

Auto Tour Route

175

Bunting Rd.

Pony Swim

Woodland Trail

Toms Cove

Chincoteague Inlet

Toms Cove Visitor Center National Park Service

Wallops Island (NASA)

Toms Cove Hook

	Refuge Office
	Visitor Center
	Point of Interest

Maryland

Virginia

WHAT TO SEE

■ **LANDSCAPE AND CLIMATE** Like all barrier islands, Assateague is dynamic, changing shape and location, constantly shifting under the prod of wind and water. This process is clearest at the refuge's south end, where Toms Cove Hook crooks a finger toward land that has been growing for much of the last century. A gently sloping beach rises to open dunes, where salt spray, sun, and the play of wind keep life to a minimum. Farther from the sea is the back dune community, a tangle of shrubs and small trees, blending into mature forests of pine and hardwoods where the ground is higher. There are extensive freshwater and brackish impoundments, and tidal creeks and marshes stretch along the inner shore of the island on Chincoteague Bay.

Chincoteague is a temperate place through most of the year, spared the worst of winter weather but subject to the heat and humidity of a Virginia summer. Spring and autumn are loveliest.

■ **PLANT LIFE** Despite its relatively small size and level terrain, Chincoteague has a number of dramatically different plant communities, each heavily influenced by the proximity of the ocean.

Open beach The open beach and foredune (the side facing the water) offer little in the way of ideal growing conditions, and only a few hardy species can survive here. One is American beach grass. Its spindly appearance belies its ability, through networks of interlocking roots, to bind the dune against the wind, anchoring it and allowing other plants to get a foothold.

Also on the foredune, late summer visitors will find the blooming sea rocket, a low wild mustard with reddish flowers; seaside goldenrod; and seaside spurge, another low, sprawling plant well suited to windy conditions.

Backdunes Over the crest of the first dune, the worst of the sea wind and salt are deflected, and a more diverse plant community can take root. In the interdune meadows and (farther in) the old backdunes, the dominant species is bayberry. Highly salt-tolerant, its "berries" (actually waxy nutlets) are an important food for migrant songbirds, including some, like tree swallows, that ordinarily eat insects.

> **COPING WITH INSECTS** Insect pests can be an annoyance anytime from early spring until the first hard frost. Ticks (including Lyme disease-bearing deer ticks) are especially common, and visitors who stray from paved paths should use repellent and regularly inspect themselves for hitchhikers. Salt-marsh mosquitoes can be fierce in summer, especially in the evening and wherever there is little breeze, such as on wooded trails. Around tidal marshes, the biting, green-headed marsh files are a particular nuisance. Beaches are generally free of biting insects, if there is a breeze.

Forest Chincoteague's forests are typical of those found on old dune systems along the mid-Atlantic coast, a mixed pine and oak community that becomes taller the farther inland you walk. The main species here is loblolly pine, a tall and graceful tree whose open crown and slightly drooping branches add a distinctly southern elegance to the horizon.

Beneath the pine canopy, scrubbier hardwoods and evergreens form thickets, a web of thorny greenbrier and poison ivy, an ever-present nuisance of coastal

Sika deer, Chincoteague NWR

woodlands. Red maple is common, as are southern red oaks, with their deeply indented, sharply pointed leaves, and water oaks, whose leaves are wedge-shaped. American holly is another abundant understory species; the female trees bear their hallmark red berries from August through winter, or until the birds finally strip the last ones away.

Tidal marshes On the bay side of Assateague Island, the last of the refuge's main plant communities—tidal marshes—stretch for miles. The marshes seem monotonous, a blanket of thick, green cordgrass broken only by meandering tidal creeks. But appearances in nature are sometimes deceiving. Tidal marshes are dynamic, one of the most productive ecosystems on earth. By way of comparison, in terms of organic production, a salt marsh produces about 10 tons of organic matter per acre per year, compared to just one and a half for a prime wheatfield.

The keystone species in the tidal marsh are two cordgrasses of the genus *Spartina*, which form mats spreading for hundreds of acres. Saltwater cordgrass, a head-high plant, grows along the edges of marshes and creeks, while salt-meadow cordgrass, a smaller plant, covers the upland parts of the marsh.

Cordgrasses are among the few kinds of vascular plants to withstand immersion in saltwater, growing where the rising tide inundates their roots twice each day. The densely packed stems filter the water, trapping sediment and detritus and building the fertile mud layers of the marsh; they also provide homes for a tremendous diversity of animal life, from fiddler crabs that burrow near the roots to seaside sparrows flitting furtively among the stems.

■ **ANIMAL LIFE** Chincoteague offers good chances for wildlife observation in almost any month of the year. A visitor in the middle of winter can watch storms of snow geese, brant, and Canada geese rise from the marshes; in spring the woods are filled with waves of migrant songbirds, along with resident species such as brown-headed nuthatches and wood ducks. Deer are common, both native white-tails and sika deer, a small, Asian relative of the American elk introduced to the Eastern Shore in the 1920s.

Birds With more than 300 species recorded and nearly 100 nesting on the refuge, birds are Chincoteague's trump card. In the warmer months, the most visible species are the waterbirds, including great, snowy, and cattle egrets; glossy ibises; and great blue, little blue, tricolored, and green-backed herons. Forster's terns hover over tidal creeks, and ospreys plunge headlong into the water, coming up with fish.

The woodlands of the refuge hold a blend of northern and southern species. Chuck-will's-widows are common (listen for them at dusk along Wildlife Loop), as are Carolina chickadees, Carolina wrens, white-eyed and red-eyed vireos, pine warblers, prairie warblers, summer tanagers, and orchard orioles.

The spring and fall migrations are perhaps the most exciting times at Chincoteague. More than 40 varieties of shorebirds, from common species like short-billed dowitchers to such rarities as curlew sandpipers, pass through the refuge, sometimes in spectacular numbers. During September and October, sharp-shinned hawks, kestrels, and merlins migrate along Assateague Island, joined by tremendous numbers of songbirds. Peregrines, a recovering species, now also nest on the refuge.

Mammals Those mammals that live on the refuge include river otter, red fox, and the endangered Delmarva fox squirrel, the last a large, pale gray subspecies found only on the Eastern Shore and reintroduced to Chincoteague in 1968.

The famous Chincoteague "wild" ponies, depending on which version of the tale you prefer, are the survivors of a Spanish shipwreck in the 1600s or (more likely) the offspring of horses pastured on the island by local residents, once a common practice. The 150 or so horses seem tame but they bite and kick. Feeding the horses (or any wildlife) is illegal. The refuge herd is owned by the local volunteer fire company—which auctions off some of the foals each July during pony-penning week (see "Seasonal Events").

Reptiles and amphibians There are no venomous snakes on the island, but Chincoteague is home to nonvenomous northern water snakes, eastern ribbon, hognose snakes, and black rat snakes. On rainy evenings the trails may come alive with thousands of Fowler's toads, and humid nights are filled with the calls of both gray and green tree frogs. Eastern painted turtles bask on floating logs, while snapping turtles float in the water.

Invertebrates Chincoteague's beach and tidal zones are exceptionally rich in invertebrate life. On the open beach, look for ghost crabs, pale as the sand itself, darting in and out of their burrows. Beach fleas (which, unlike true fleas, are not insects and do not bite) are small arthropods about an inch long; they leap wildly when the mats of dead seaweed that they hide under are disturbed. More odd is the mole crab, a burrowing species built like an inch-long egg; its molted carapace, or shell, is commonly found by beachcombers.

Because Chincoteague's sand beaches slope so gently, there are few tide pools to explore, but the waves constantly bring in relics of the life hidden just beyond the surf line: the large, whorled shells of channeled whelks (and their

Channeled whelk

strange egg cases, looking like necklaces of parchment disks), shells from clams, cockles, and scallops, even the bones of whales and dolphins. Shell collecting is permitted.

ACTIVITIES

■ **CAMPING:** Camping is not allowed on Chincoteague NWR itself, but there are a number of private campgrounds on neighboring Chincoteague Island (call Chincoteague Island Chamber of Commerce, 757/336-6161) as well as at nearby Pocomoke River State Park in Maryland (410/632-2566).

■ **SWIMMING:** Chincoteague's ocean surf is a swimmer's delight, while the mud-bottomed bayside and coves are best avoided. Currents can be tricky, and swimmers should use the life-guarded beach by Toms Cove Visitor Center, where parking, changing stalls, showers, and toilets are available. Inflatable mats and tubes are prohibited.

■ **WILDLIFE OBSERVATION:** Songbird migration from early April through late May brings flycatchers, warblers, and vireo. Wooded areas of Wildlife Loop and Woodland Trail are among the best locations to find these birds. The "autumn" shorebird migration starts in late July and August, with a secondary migration of immature shorebirds in September. Wash Flats is one of the best locations.

Wetlands at dusk, Chincoteague NWR

Large numbers of migrant monarch butterflies pass through Chincoteague in late August and September, drifting along the dunes by the dozens and even hundreds. The fall waterfowl migration begins with teal in September and runs through the late-autumn arrival of snow geese, Canada geese, and brant.

■ **PHOTOGRAPHY:** Unlike many refuges, Chincoteague has no photo blinds, but it is nonetheless one of the best places in the East for wildlife photography. Early morning offers the best lighting conditions, greatest wildlife activity, and fewest people. Using a car as a blind, cruise slowly along Beach Road, watching for wading birds such as yellow-crowned night-heron.

Wildlife Loop is always productive for photos, although it pays to be out at daybreak before the crowds of joggers and bikers descend. After 3 p.m. the route is open to vehicles, although along most of the loop the light angle is wrong for photography in the evening.

■ **HIKES AND WALKS:** Hiking trails include Woodland Trail (1.6 mi.) and popular Wildlife Loop (3.2 mi.). Both are also open to bicycling, and Wildlife Loop is open to vehicles after 3 p.m. The easy Lighthouse Trail is just 0.25 mi. long, and there is a short nature trail near the Toms Cove amphitheater.

■ **SEASONAL EVENTS:** The refuge and National Seashore offer guided walks and tours, including morning bird walks, explorations of the beach and tidal marsh, surf fishing and crabbing demonstrations, lectures on whales and Chincoteague history. A concessionaire also runs a 15-mile auto Wildlife Safari. July: Pony penning (last week); auction last Wednesday of July. The horses are corralled on the refuge, then herded across the channel to Chincoteague Island. After the auction, those not sold are herded back to the refuge. October: National Wildlife Refuge Week; annual Oyster Festival. November: Waterfowl Week, during Thanksgiving week; displays, art, nature activities.

■ **PUBLICATIONS:** Free refuge pamphlets and brochures, including a color guide to the refuge and the National Seashore; a bird checklist; tips on crabbing, clamming, and surf fishing; information on the pony herd.

Assateague Island, by William Amos (published by the National Park Service and part of the National Park Handbook series), describes the natural and human history of the island, including Chincoteague NWR.

HUNTING AND FISHING There is both surf- and fresh-water-fishing allowed on the refuge. Bank fishing and crabbing (for **blue crabs**) are permitted in Swan's Cove Pool; however, boating is not allowed in any of the refuge pools. Anglers commonly find **black drum**, **bluefish**, **channel bass**, **fluke**, and **weakfish**. There are also numerous hunting opportunities at Chincoteague NWR: a **goose** hunt in Sept., **duck** hunting from Oct. through Jan., and a **deer** hunt (white-tailed and sika) in Dec. Contact the refuge for information on permits and regulations.

Eastern Shore of Virginia NWR

Cape Charles, Virginia

Royal terns

In the eyes of British explorer and colonist Captain John Smith, "it was a faire Bay compassed but for the mouth with fruitful and delightsome land. Heaven and earth never agreed better to frame a place for man's habitation." Captain Smith was referring to the southern tip of what we now call the Delmarva Peninsula, the great arm of land that separates Chesapeake Bay from the Atlantic Ocean and contains the eastern reaches of three states: Delaware, Maryland, and Virginia. Rimmed by sandy barrier islands that cradle fertile bays and salt marshes, the southernmost portion of Delmarva is indeed a fair place, but not just for people. It is here, in and around the Eastern Shore of Virginia NWR in autumn, that migratory birds by the thousands, even hundreds of thousands, gather to feed and rest before crossing the waters of the Chesapeake.

HISTORY

Farming has long been the key occupation on the fertile agricultural land of the Eastern Shore. So has working the water; the legendary watermen of Chesapeake Bay, generation upon generation, have for years earned a living oystering, crabbing, and fishing. The land that the refuge occupies was privately owned until shortly before World War II, when, because of its strategic location, it was taken by the federal government to create Fort John Custis. Large bunkers housed 16-inch guns to protect naval facilities at Virginia Beach and Norfolk. Some of the bunkers are still visible on the refuge. After the war it became Cape Charles Air Force Base, which closed in 1980.

In the early 1980s, recreational development began to spread in the area, threatening migratory staging areas used by birds. The Air Force transferred 180 acres in 1984 to the U.S. Fish & Wildlife Service to create the refuge as a safe house for avian migrants. Today, Eastern Shore covers about 700 acres. Though a small property by NWR standards, Eastern Shore is a magnet: More than 125,000 people visit here each year, a portion of them hunters.

A larger, undeveloped refuge on Fishermans Island, a half-mile south of the mainland, was also assigned to headquarters at Eastern Shore for management.

GETTING THERE

Eastern Shore NWR is located east of the north toll plaza of the Chesapeake Bay Bridge Tunnel and US 13. Take VA 600 east for about 0.25 mi. The refuge entrance is on the right.

■ **SEASON:** Refuge open year-round.

■ **HOURS:** General refuge: dawn to dusk. Visitor Center: April–Nov., 9 a.m.– 4 p.m., daily; Dec. and March, 10 a.m.–2 p.m. daily; Jan. and Feb., Fri.–Sun., 10 a.m.–2 p.m.

■ **FEES:** None.

■ **ADDRESS:** Eastern Shore of Virginia NWR, 5003 Hallett Circle, Cape Charles, VA 23310

■ **TELEPHONE:** 757/331-2760

TOURING EASTERN SHORE

■ **BY AUTOMOBILE:** Hallett Circle is a loop road used to reach headquarters and other refuge facilities. It is not an official auto tour but passes by some of the key wildlife viewing areas.

■ **BY FOOT:** There are two trails at Eastern Shore. Butterfly Trail, starting at the Visitor Center, provides a walk of about .5 mi. (one-way) through open fields where butterflies frequent the wildflowers. Wildflower Trail, starting from the parking lot on Fitchett Road, makes a loop of about .5 mi., passing by a WWII bunker and a salt marsh.

■ **BY BICYCLE:** Cyclists may use Fitchett Road and portions of Hallett Circle.

■ **BY CANOE, KAYAK, OR BOAT:** There is no boating at this refuge.

WHAT TO SEE

■ **LANDSCAPE AND CLIMATE** This is a low, flat coastal landscape that merges with salt marshes laced by tidal creeks. It speaks of the sea, which surrounds it on three sides. The weather here is moderated by the ocean but still can be highly variable. Summer days are often hot and muggy. But sea breezes usually

FISHERMANS ISLAND As islands go, Fishermans is a newborn. Sand and gravel built up around the wreck of a cargo vessel in the early 1800s, and the island gradually rose from the sea. During World War I, Fishermans Island served as an artillery bastion, designed to protect the Chesapeake from German incursions. It remained a military base through World War II. As early as 1933, however, the island's environmental value was recognized. The War Department sanctioned its use as a bird sanctuary as well as a military installation. Today, Fishermans Island covers almost 2,000 acres, all of which is national wildlife refuge land, used primarily as a nesting and staging ground for aquatic birds. Eastern Shore NWR headquarters can schedule tours of the island from October to March. There is no other access to the island.

keep the ambient temperature no higher than the mid-80s. From spring to winter, ocean storms can lash the area with heavy rain. Winter brings the occasional ice and snow, but daytime temperatures can also rise as high as 60 degrees. Rarely do temperatures drop into the single digits.

■ **PLANT LIFE** The climatic influence of the sea is evident on surveying the region's plant life. Maritime forest is the dominant plant community. The sea also affects the woodlands hereabouts, called maritime forest. The woods here are very different from those on the mainland, which typically contain a large variety of hardwoods as well as pine. The climax forest here is loblolly pine, but its only hardwoods are oaks, more tolerant of wind and salt spray than most deciduous trees. As if to express its dominance, the sea has stunted many of the trees on Fishermans Island.

Dunes Only highly specialized plants can live in the low sand dunes that front the ocean beach. These are hardy species, able to combat wind, waves, and salt spray. Among them: sea rocket, Russian thistle, and American beach grass. In a sense, they create their own habitat. They anchor the sand in place against the depredations of the sea. If they die, so do the dunes, which are swept away. Eastern Shore's dunes are closed to the public.

Tidal marshes On shallow flats, shielded from heavy wave action, marshes dominated by cordgrasses take hold. Closest to the sea is the salt-marsh cordgrass.

Snowy egret

On the upper edges of the marsh is the salt-meadow cordgrass, often called salt hay. The marshes farthest from the sea also contain black needlerush and salt grass.

Shrubland Behind the dunes and marshes grow plant communities of shrubs. Here you will find bayberry, wax myrtle, and groundsel. The leaves of many such plants are tough skinned, holding in moisture (as succulent plants do in the desert) and resisting the salty sea wind.

Woodlands As distance from the sea increases and ground level rises, small trees, such as black cherry, appear. Further inland, loblolly pines, with a holly understory, take over, then mix with scattered oaks, mostly live oak, which reaches its northernmost coastal range here.

Freshwater marshes and ponds Small marshes and ponds have been created here to increase habitat diversity. Cattails and sedges are among the plants most easy to see.

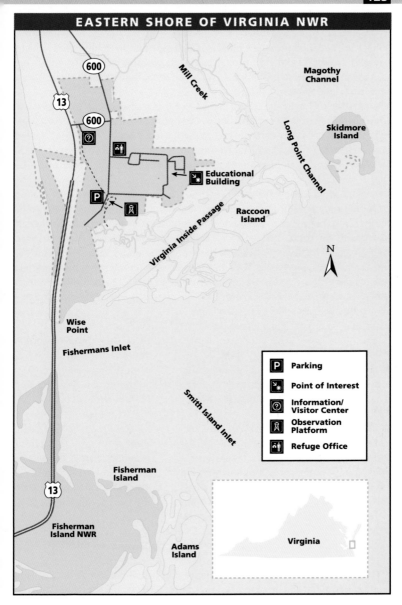

EASTERN SHORE OF VIRGINIA NWR

Mill Creek

Magothy Channel

Long Point Channel

Skidmore Island

600

13

600

⊘

Educational Building

Raccoon Island

Virginia Inside Passage

P

Wise Point

Fishermans Inlet

Smith Island Inlet

N

P	Parking
☀	Point of Interest
⊘	Information/ Visitor Center
♙	Observation Platform
⚥	Refuge Office

Fisherman Island

13

Fisherman Island NWR

Adams Island

Virginia

■ **ANIMAL LIFE** At Eastern Shore, a kind of land's end, creatures from land meet and often interact with those of the sea. Raccoons forage on beaches for crabs, mussels, and clams. Bats wing through the air at night, gulls by day.

Birds Almost 300 species of birds—amazingly, about half of those listed in North America—have been seen here. The migrants are many. In the late fall and early winter, American woodcock, considered by scientists to be a shorebird but really an uplander, zoom out of the woodlands at dusk to search for worms in the fields. Songbirds are a special attraction here, primarily in spring and fall. Among the many you can listen for are American redstart, common yellowthroat, and yellow-rumped warbler (the latter appear fall through winter, by the thousands). During late summer and fall, hawks, such as the kestrel and sharp-shinned, wing through. Spring and fall bring whimbrel, short-billed dowitchers, red knots, sanderlings, yellowlegs, and semipalmated plovers. Come spring, the long-legged waders arrive. Snowy egrets and great egrets, their white plumage looking like snowballs against the green marsh vegetation. Great blue herons, unlike the other egrets, stay here year-round to breed and feed.

Mammals It is night at Eastern Shore. And it is suppertime. A big brown bat homes in on a mosquito. A red fox creeps through the meadow in search of a tasty vole. A white-tailed deer munches on browse at a forest edge. Visitors may not see these vignettes, but, during daylight touring hours, they have a good chance of seeing a deer or coyote or even an otter slipping through the quiet water of a tidal creek.

Reptiles and amphibians Frogs most likely to be observed here are the green frog and the bullfrog. During spring and summer, and into fall until the cold weather hits, they may be seen floating in freshwaters or squatting in the mud at water's edge. Hidden in the woodlands and scrub are several species of tree frogs: spring peepers, the gray tree frog, and the chorus frog among them. Turtles are the reptiles that are most evident here. In brackish marshes, snapping turtles thrive. Red-bellied turtles and painted turtles bask on logs and rocks in freshwater areas. Do not be surprised to see a snake on the trail or near the water. This is prime habitat for the northern water snake, the black rat snake, and the coastal plain milk snake.

ACTIVITIES

■ **CAMPING:** Although there is no camping on the refuge, you may camp at nearby Kiptopeake State Park. Contact them at 757/331-2267.

■ **WILDLIFE OBSERVATION:** The interpretive trail takes you through woodlands and to the edges of the marsh. This is a fine spot to see aquatic birds. Throughout the year, look for bobwhite quail along trail edges. Where you see one, you will probably see many. Bobwhites gather in groups, called coveys. Even if scattered, they come together within minutes. During the spring and summer, check osprey nesting platforms to see these great birds of prey and their young.

HUNTING AND FISHING
There is no fishing in the refuge. However, the surrounding waters draw anglers from all over.

The refuge has limited bowhunting and shotgun **deer** hunts (by lottery), from Oct. to Dec. Contact the refuge for details, exact dates for each season, and permits needed.

■ **PHOTOGRAPHY:** On the interpretive trail, just off Fitchett Road, there is a photography blind and an observation platform. They overlook a two-acre freshwater pond that is frequently busy with large numbers of waterfowl.

■ **SEASONAL EVENTS:** The eastern side (of Chesapeake Bay) is the most legendary waterfowling area in the United States. Since the 1800s, waterfowlers have flocked here to hunt. Many towns hereabouts have annual waterfowl festivals, featuring exhibits of waterfowl art, particularly decoys. The Visitor Center at Eastern Shore NWR has an exhibit of decoys and other bird carvings as well as other handicrafts by the region's artists. Interactive exhibits highlight four Eastern Shore habitats. The Eastern Shore Birding Festival happens in October.

■ **PUBLICATIONS:** The Visitor Center offers pamphlets and species lists.

Great Dismal Swamp NWR
Suffolk, Virginia

Swamp forest, Great Dismal Swamp NWR

Legends haunt the impenetrable recesses of the flooded forests, marshes, and bogs of this wilderness on the low-lying Atlantic Coastal Plain, just south of Portsmouth, Virginia. It's one of the largest swamps in the United States north of Florida.

Lore of the Nansemond Indians has it that the lake at its center was created by a firebird, which some historians speculate may have been a meteor impact. The interior of the swamp was also a haven for fugitive slaves seeking freedom and lawbreakers on the run.

But not all those who disappeared into this foreboding morass did so willingly. In 1665, North Carolina governor William Drummond entered the swamp on a hunting expedition with a group of friends and soon became lost. Drummond slogged through the wet wilderness to emerge at the lake that now bears his name, yet he was the only one to emerge. The others were lost in muck, mire, and time.

Today, the swamp's mysterious allure still beckons. Although Great Dismal Swamp is not a place for wandering about heedlessly, visitors need not worry about adding their names to its legends lost.

HISTORY

Native Americans occupied the area around Great Dismal Swamp 13,000 years ago, but by the mid-1600s only the Nansemond people, the descendants of whom still inhabit the edges of the swamp, remained here. To many early Americans, except for George Washington and some others, the swamp was a hell, alive with venomous serpents, prowled by bears, a water-logged maze of tangled vegetation that should be drained and converted to agriculture. Indeed, Washington founded a company that logged and drained parts of the swamp. A drainage ditch, 5 miles long, still carries the first president's name. Attempts were made over two centuries to vanquish the swamp, its tangled growth tamed for agriculture, its massive trees logged. The swamp survived it all, with a little help from, ironically, a major logging company, as well as the U.S. Fish & Wildlife Service. In 1973, the Union Camp Company donated 49,100 acres of the swamp to The Nature Conservancy who then convey it to the the U.S. Fish & Wildlife Service. The next year, the refuge was established. It has since grown to over 109,000 acres and crosses the border into North Carolina.

GETTING THERE

From Suffolk, VA, take US 13 south to VA 32, go south for another 4.5 mi., then follow signs to the refuge.

■ **SEASON:** Refuge open year-round.

■ **HOURS:** General refuge open daily from a half-hour before sunrise to a half-hour after sunset. Headquarters open Mon.–Fri., 7 a.m.–3:30 p.m. The Washington Ditch entrance is open April 1–Sept. 30, 6:30 a.m.–8p.m; Oct. 1–March 31, 6:30 a.m.–5 p.m.

■ **FEES:** None.

■ **ADDRESS:** Great Dismal Swamp NWR, P.O. Box 349, Suffolk, VA 23439-0349

■ **TELEPHONE:** 757/986-3705

LEGENDS AND LORE OF GREAT DISMAL SWAMP Colonial and later southern society built around it. Farms and houses rimmed it. The bastions of civilization were secure, but their inhabitants dreaded the swamp. Great Dismal is a swamp in every sense of the word, a dark, dank wilderness. Here the forgotten children found a soggy refuge. Escaped slaves, fleeing plantation masters, made shingles from the wood of cedar trees to pay for their freedom. Dred, the runaway slave in Harriet Beecher Stowe's *Uncle Tom's Cabin*, hid in the swamp until he could lead other slaves to freedom. The swamp was a refuge for impoverished whites as well, those shunning civilization's advance, and for wild creatures facing the same pressures. For them all, the Great Dismal Swamp was refuge, much as it is today for the wild creatures who inhabit it.

TOURING GREAT DISMAL SWAMP

■ **BY AUTOMOBILE:** Refuge roads are not open to automobiles.

■ **BY FOOT:** Swamp roads make for good walking. Remember, if you're going on a long trek, this is still *wilderness*. Ask at headquarters for suggested routes. Caution: Three venomous snakes inhabit the refuge, the cottonmouth and canebrake rattlesnake, which are highly dangerous, and the copperhead. There is also a short Boardwalk Trail located at the Washington Ditch entrance.

■ **BY BICYCLE:** There are approximately 150 miles of unpaved roads throughout the refuge which are open to hiking and biking only. Visitors must stay on the designated trails/roads. The roads are open to bikers. Washington Ditch Road is recommended. Mountain bikers can go for it on some of the more rugged roads, even if there are no mountains here. Hikers and bikers must stay on designated trails.

■ **BY CANOE, KAYAK, OR BOAT:** Boating is permitted year-round on Lake Drummond. Access is from Highway 17 on a ramp on the Feeder Ditch, which connects the lake with Dismal Swamp Canal. Caution: Boats must be portaged

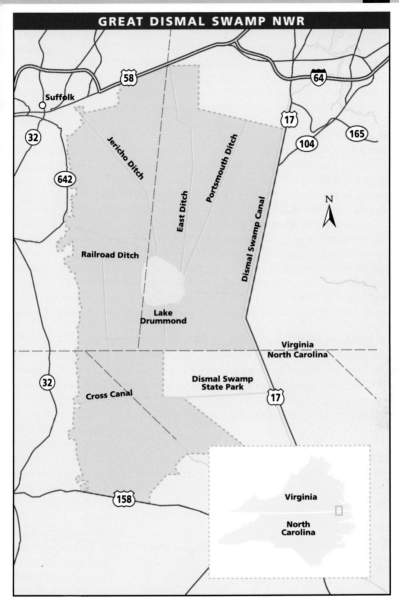

(about 75 feet) around a water-control structure near the lake. Motors are restricted to 25 hp.

WHAT TO SEE

■ **LANDSCAPE AND CLIMATE** Geologically, Great Dismal Swamp is almost as mysterious as the legends that shroud it. The swamp probably took shape millions of years ago, but the processes that built it are not precisely understood. Swamps form in low-lying areas, and Great Dismal, 25 feet above sea level at most, is bounded on the west by a ridge that is twice that altitude. The soil of the swamp is topped by a layer of peat. Beneath it is clay, which thwarts drainage of water, and peat soaks up moisture like a sponge. The combination, by any geologist's measure, makes for a swamp. Lake Drummond, 3,100 acres with an average depth of 6 feet, was probably caused by a long-standing fire (started by a "firebird": lightning, meteor, or something else) that burned peat down into a bowl.

The weather in Dismal Swamp is generally fine in spring, fall, and winter. Summer makes the swamp truly dismal, with hot, muggy weather that brings out the flies, mosquitoes, and ticks. Winter temperatures are moderate.

■ PLANT LIFE

Forests Deciduous and coniferous forests here have an eye-pleasing variety, including areas dominated by loblolly pine, Atlantic white cedar, bald cypress, maples, black gum, sweet gum, oaks, and poplars. Red maple, invasive and swamp loving, is conquering much of the forest where the original trees have been logged. Water is the lifeblood of the swamp. Water is being conserved and managed by placing water control structures in the ditches.

Open wetlands The freshwater wetlands of the swamp, diminished by former human activities but now being renewed by refuge managers, contain sedges, rushes, water lilies, and, in secret bogs, the squishy, verdant carpet of sphagnum moss. Even in times before the swamp was despoiled, however, the shade of trees kept sunny wetlands to a minimum. A sunlit marsh, to the human mind, is not essentially dismal. A swamp darkened by gnarled trees can be downright spooky.

■ ANIMAL LIFE

Great Dismal Swamp differs from most other refuges on the Atlantic Coastal Plain in that it does not border on the sea and lacks vast horizons. The view is masked by trees and tangles. Even so, patience and a curious eye can discover many types of wildlife, including some that sun in the wide-open places of other refuges.

Birds Thousands of waterfowl can be seen on Lake Drummond during the winter months. The 200-plus bird species recorded in Dismal Swamp refuge overall, and the 93 that nest here, are the stuff that makes an impressive birder's life list. The forests bring in the warblers, including Swainson's and Wayne's, which in this area reach the northern end of their ranges. Barred owls and pileated woodpeckers, creatures that like big woods, can be spotted among the big trees. The barred owl is one of the few owls active by day. Birding is best here during spring

White-tailed deer

migration from April to June, when the greatest diversity of species (particularly warblers) occurs.

Mammals Like the legends of the swamp, the bobcat slips through the darkness, seldom seen but sometimes heard when its yowls pierce the night during mating season. Black bears are here, too, but not as eager to greet humans as they are in national parks where garbage and illegal handouts give them fast food. Look in streams and open marshes for otters. Early in the morning, a mink might be seen at waterside. White-tailed deer abound.

Reptiles and amphibians This is herp heaven. More than 50 species of turtles, lizards, salamanders, toads, and frogs inhabit the refuge. The 3- to 5-inch spotted turtle, its black shell dotted with yellow, is more commonly seen here than in many other places. Recently, alligators have been seen close to the refuge.

Invertebrates Great Dismal Swamp has so many butterflies that official annual counts by aficionados of these handsome insects are sometimes done here. Take your pick: zebra swallowtails, pearl crescents, and viceroys, among others.

Boardwalk Trail, Great Dismal Swamp NWR

ACTIVITIES

■ **WILDLIFE OBSERVATION AND PHOTOGRAPHY:** Birding is best in the swamp from April to June, when warblers, blackbirds, and robins swarm about. Soaring overhead in late winter are red-shouldered and red-tailed hawks. The best chance to see a black bear is in early June, when the breeding season peaks.

You may need some sophisticated photography skills to do well here in the muted light or when shooting from a sunny area into a darker one. There are no established photography towers or bird blinds. You will need to improvise a photography blind, and your car may be as good as anything else. A good photographer can stop along the roads at any number of handsome places and catch the essence of this swampy wilderness.

■ **HIKES AND WALKS:** The 0.75-mile Boardwalk Trail is located at the Washington Ditch entrance, off White Marsh Road (Rte. 642). This handicapped-accessible trail runs through forest and marsh, representative of Great Dismal habitats.

■ **PUBLICATIONS:** Refuge pamphlets.

Mason Neck NWR
Potomac River Complex, Woodbridge, Virginia

Wetland and woodland meadow, Mason Neck NWR

Fewer than 20 miles from the nation's capital, along the Potomac River, the country's national symbol, its numbers dwindling dramatically, found refuge. Mason Neck NWR, now the core of the Potomac NWR Complex, was a haven for live bald eagles when virtually the only others in the area were emblems on law-enforcement badges and in paintings on the walls of public buildings. Today, many eagles winter in the refuge and on surrounding public lands; during the late winter and spring, some breed there, and the number of eagles that set up house may well increase.

The Potomac River Complex includes Occoquan Bay NWR (see separate entry), a budding flower in the refuge system, and Featherstone NWR, closed to the public but not to the aquatic birds that use its precious wetlands. The complex has wetlands galore; Mason Neck includes the largest freshwater marsh in northern Virginia, covering about 200 acres. Add to that 2,000 acres of mature hardwood forest and a half-dozen miles of riverfront at Mason Neck alone, and the value of the Potomac River Complex is obvious.

HISTORY

The eagles were there long before Virginia patriot and statesman George Mason built a plantation at Mason Neck in 1775. Eagles were driven away the next century by logging, which continued into the early 1900s and decimated the forests. By the 1960s, trees had regenerated, but residential development from nearby Washington, DC, posed another threat. Concerned citizens, conservation groups, and government agencies fought back, and, with the purchase of 845 acres, Mason Neck NWR was founded in 1969.

GETTING THERE

Refuge: Head south from Washington, DC, along Rte. 1 to a left turn at 242

(Gunston Rd.). After 4 mi., turn right on High Point Rd., which divides the refuge and a state wildlife management area, both marked by signs. Headquarters (Potomac River Complex): Rte. 1 south to Woodbridge becomes Jefferson Davis Hwy., 2 mi. away. Office in Prince William Plaza, Woodbridge, on Jefferson Davis Hwy.

■ **SEASON:** Refuge open year-round.

■ **HOURS:** Trails open sunrise to sunset. Headquarters open 8 a.m.–4:30 p.m., weekdays. Visitors must stay on designated trails and roads.

■ **FEES:** Free entry.

■ **ADDRESS:** Mason Neck NWR, 14344 Jefferson Davis Hwy., Woodbridge, VA 22191

■ **TELEPHONE:** 703/490-4979

TOURING MASON NECK

■ **BY AUTOMOBILE:** There is no auto route within the refuge.

■ **BY FOOT:** There are two short hiking trails, one leading through forest and marsh, the other essentially all marshland.

■ **BY BICYCLE:** Bikes are allowed on a handful of paved roads that traverse the refuge.

■ **BY CANOE, KAYAK, OR BOAT:** No facilities for boating within the refuge, but the Potomac River is open to navigation.

WHAT TO SEE

■ **LANDSCAPE AND CLIMATE** Mason Neck is just that, a peninsula jutting out into the Potomac, where the river begins to widen toward its mouth at Chesapeake Bay. The refuge is located on what might be described as the "head of the neck," where it broadens laterally and presents a face of fertile marsh to the main stream. The riverside has relatively mild winters with occasional snows, and hot, often muggy summers.

■ **PLANT LIFE**
Freshwater marsh Mason Neck is far enough upriver from the mouth of the Potomac River so that its marshes, although influenced by tides, are fresh. Great Marsh, the main freshwater wetland at Mason Neck, is nearly pristine. Wild rice, a key waterfowl food, raises its tasseled head here. Pickerelweed shows off blooms of blue, while bulrushes and cattails grow tall. Around the margins of the water, look for the glorious red blossoms of cardinal flower, thriving in soggy ground.

Green-winged teal

Forest The woodlands of Mason Neck were intensively logged during the

MASON NECK NWR, POTOMAC RIVER COMPLEX

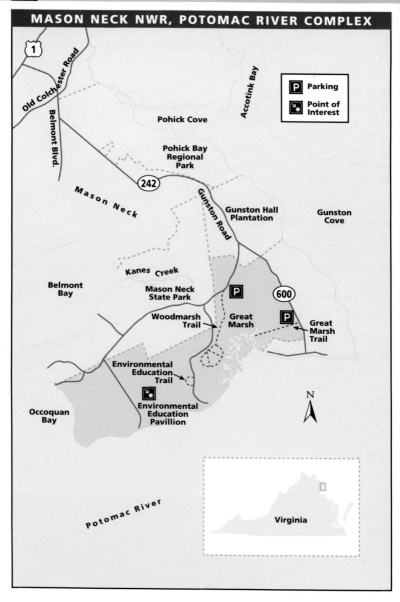

19th- and early 20th centuries. They have since regenerated into a forest of mixed hardwoods, dominated by hickories and oaks. Scattered among the hardwood are pines, which were more numerous in prelogging days.

■ **ANIMAL LIFE** A plentiful variety of animals can be seen at Mason Neck year-round, although the cast changes seasonally.

■ **Birds** When it comes to birds at Mason Neck, what you see depends on when you visit. But whenever you come here, you will see them in abundance. During April bald eaglets are hatching and great blue herons are courting. Teal are here momentarily and then are gone, headed north on their spring migration. If you like baby birds, visit in May, when wood ducks, black ducks, and Canada geese broods are learning to feed in the marsh. In June, look for eaglets setting out on their first flights. Remember that young bald eagles do not develop a white head and tail until they are from three to five years of age. Fall is one of the best times for birding at Mason Neck. Resident aquatic birds mix with migrants. Herons, egrets, teals, mallards, and black ducks all abound in this season.

Mammals Beavers, holed up for much of the winter, get busy in spring, rebuilding their dams and lodges. Because beavers are primarily nocturnal, the best times to see them are early morning or just before the refuge closes at sunset. At any time, however, you can see evidence of their industry: dams and lodges of sticks and mud, tree stumps gnawed into sharpened stakes. Beavers were logging here long before people tried it. Also check for large burrows in banks of streams. Like muskrats, common at the refuge, beavers sometimes live in burrows as well as lodges. Woodsmen often call those that do so "bank beavers."

Other mammals living on the refuge include red fox, weasels, mink, and, in high numbers, white-tailed deer. The forest floor in the refuge is relatively open, due to browsing deer.

HUNTING AND FISHING
There are two four-day shotgun **white-tailed deer** hunts on the refuge each year, one in Nov. and one in Dec. The refuge holds a lottery each fall for hunters who wish to take part in the hunts; contact the refuge office in Aug. to be a part of the lottery. There is no fishing on the refuge.

Reptiles and amphibians From spring to fall a keen observer can see turtles, painted and snapping turtles among them, and bullfrogs and green frogs. Water snakes and black rat snakes are common at Mason Neck.

ACTIVITIES

■ **WILDLIFE OBSERVATION AND PHOTOGRAPHY:** Woodmarsh Trail offers good views of beaver habitat and waterfowl. Keep an eye out for otters. Great Marsh Trail is a direct route through forest to the marsh that bears its name. It is a good place to see immature eagles roosting in trees.

There are no special facilities for photographers, but both trails provide good opportunities.

■ **HIKES AND WALKS:** Woodmarsh Trail, 0.75 miles from the park entrance, is a 3-mile round-trip, and, as the name suggests, it runs through both forest and marshland. Great Marsh Trail, 1.5 miles from the park entrance, is less than a mile, one-way. Both trailheads are at parking lots.

Besides the trails, a few walkable roads go through the refuge. Anchorage Road runs from High Point Road to the river's edge.

■ **PUBLICATIONS:** Refuge brochure and walking trails pamphlets.

Occoquan Bay NWR
Potomac River Complex, Woodbridge, Virginia

American kestrel

Undisturbed native grasslands are precious anywhere in North America, but nowhere more so than along the Atlantic seaboard, where forest rather than field has dominated the landscape since the end of the last Ice Age. This is what makes Occoquan Bay National Wildlife Refuge, though small and very new, especially appealing—particularly for birders. Occoquan Bay refuge, about 700 acres, embraces one of the largest native grasslands remaining in northern Virginia. As a result, it attracts flocks of birds who sing, nest, and feed among verdant meadows, planted not by humans but by nature. Grassland, however, is not the only habitat at Occoquan. Woodlands and freshwater marshes form other interesting parts of the refuge along Occoquan Bay, in the Potomac River, about 20 miles south of Washington, DC.

HISTORY

Occoquan Bay NWR is located on the opposite shores of the bay from Mason Neck NWR, which with Occoquan, is part of the Potomac River NWR Complex. It was established in June 1998 when 586 acres of land from a former research facility of the U.S. Army—a top-secret spot in its day—were combined with the 64 acres of the now defunct Marmusco NWR. The refuge will be in a development stage for many years, so regulations and permitted activities are in a state of flux.

GETTING THERE

From Rte. 1 in Woodbridge, head east on Dawson Beach Rd., which dead-ends at the complex of old buildings that were once part of the military facility. One of these structures is undergoing renovation and will serve as the Visitor Contact Station.

■ **SEASON:** Initially, the refuge was open weekends from February through April. This will be expanded, so check before visiting.

- **HOURS:** General refuge hours are presently variable, but during daylight. Best to check headquarters, open from 8 a.m.–4:30 p.m., weekdays.
- **FEES:** None at present, but eventually a charge will be implemented.
- **ADDRESS:** Potomac River NWR Complex, Occoquan Bay NWR, 14344 Jefferson Davis Hwy., Woodbridge, VA 22191
- **TELEPHONE:** 703/490-4979

TOURING OCCOQUAN BAY

- **BY AUTOMOBILE:** An auto-tour route will be available to visitors in spring 2000.
- **BY FOOT:** Visitors on foot may tour on compacted gravel roads once used by guards patrolling the military installation. There is a 2-mile loop, starting at the parking lot with Fox Rd. Along the way, Easy Rd. branches off Fox Rd. Both lead to Deephole Point Rd., which runs along the river.
- **BY BICYCLE:** Bicycles will also be allowed on the future auto-tour roads.
- **BY CANOE, KAYAK, OR BOAT:** No boating access on the refuge, but the Potomac River nearby is navigable.

WHAT TO SEE

- **LANDSCAPE AND CLIMATE** Occoquan's climate is similar to Washington's to the north, with a few cold snaps and snows in winter and summer days sultry enough to make bureaucrats loosen their ties. Typical of a place on the water's edge, the refuge is flat. You will not have to hike up hills here.

- **PLANT LIFE**

Grasslands Occoquan's grasslands are the realm of grama grasses, such as big bluestem, the same group that ruled the western prairies—and still exists there in patches. Oxeye daisies and purple milkweed bloom, and field thistles lend color to the meadows.

Oxeye daisy

Forests Woodlands are composed mostly of hardwoods, such as pin, white, and scarlet oaks, as well as hickories, which provide nuts for resident squirrels, deer, turkeys, and raccoons. The forest floor nurtures jack-in-the-pulpit and a variety of ferns, including Christmas ferns. "Jack" loves damp woods and swamps; it's an upright but shy flower, hiding under large leaves. He can grow from 1 to 3 feet and will show off shiny red berries in late summer and fall. "Jack" wears a curved, ridged hood; the "pulpit," with an erect club beneath it, is in mottled browns and greens.

Marshes Pickerelweed, sedges, and rushes adorn the marshes. Duckweed covers quiet pockets of water with a carpet of green, and wild rice beckons the waterfowl that flock to the refuge's multiple food sources.

■ ANIMAL LIFE

Birds Go to Occoquan for birds. Compacted into this little place are more than 200 species, including some that are not easy to find elsewhere in the region. The bubbling call of the bobolink, the piercing whistles of the meadowlark, and the buzzing of the Savannah sparrow rise from the grasslands from spring to fall. The grasslands also attract kestrels, in abundance; harriers, winging over the marsh, patrol the meadows on outstretched wings. Aquatic birds abound. Typical species found along the water include dunlin, king rails, herons, and glossy ibises. In the woodland, great horned and short-eared owls sleep during the day, to prowl at night.

Mammals Given the limited hours the refuge is open and the secret behavior of mammals, this is not the best place to go if mammals are your bag. But keep an eye out. You might see an otter in the marsh or a white-tailed deer at forest's edge.

ACTIVITIES

■ **WILDLIFE OBSERVATION AND PHOTOGRAPHY:** The roads that are open provide an opportunity for visitors to observe grasslands, wet forests, and wetlands. There are no special facilities for nature photography.

■ **HIKES AND WALKS:** The old military patrol roads see very little car traffic and make for leisurely walks. No jogging or running is allowed on the refuge.

■ **PUBLICATIONS:** General-information maps are available at refuge headquarters.

Presquile NWR
Chester, Virginia

Eastern bluebird

William Randolph came to this small peninsula in the James River in 1660 to farm. Before he died, he was one of Virginia's most prominent personages—and he planted more than crops. He founded a family tree whose trunk and branches later included some of the most prominent names in the Old South, indeed, in America. Among them are Thomas Jefferson and Robert E. Lee.

People today come to Presquile largely for an easy view of bald eagles. And getting there is half the fun. The only way to reach this island refuge, which lies in the middle of the James River, is by ferry, actually a barge. If you call ahead to arrange for ferry service (free), you will be among the lucky 1,700 or so people who visit this small gem each year.

HISTORY

Presquile has been known by many different names. It was called Turkey Island in the 1600s. During the Civil War, it was nicknamed "Turkey Point" or "Turkey Point Neck." Its official name, Presque Isle, a variation of the French term for "almost an island." It was not an island until the 1930s, however, when the U.S. Army Corps of Engineers cut a canal between the peninsula and the mainland to facilitate navigational traffic going up and down the river, for shipping purposes. The island became a refuge in 1953, bequeathed to the federal government by its owner, Dr. A. D. Williams.

Presquile is one of a series of small refuges in the 90-mile stretch of the Rappahannock Complex of NWRs, minor properties along the James and Rappahannock rivers. There are four properties, totalling almost 3,500 acres, on the Rappahannock between Port Royal and Tappahannock. Presquile is on the James River, as is the James River NWR. Most of these are off-limits to the public but a haven for wildlife.

GETTING THERE

Presquile is southeast of Richmond and 5 mi. north of Hopewell. From Exit 61 on I-95, follow VA 10 to Allied Rd. (VA 27), take a left onto Allied, then go 4.5 mi. to a left-hand turn at a chain-link fence; from there it is 0.3 mi. to the ferry landing. The ferry operates by request. Call refuge headquarters at least one week ahead of time. Groups of up to about 60 people can be accommodated. However, a trip will be made even if only one person requests passage. A refuge representative will accompany visitors on the island, assuring that no one will be stranded and miss the return trip. The crossing to the island is about 100 yds.

■ **SEASON:** Refuge open year-round.

■ **HOURS:** Refuge and headquarters: open 7:30 a.m.–4 p.m., weekdays only. The headquarters is about 10 miles south of the refuge proper, in close proximity to the Prince George County Courthouse, down Courthouse Rd.

■ **FEES:** None.

■ **ADDRESS:** Rappahannock Complex, P.O. Box 189, Prince George, VA 22191

■ **TELEPHONE:** 804/733-8042

TOURING PRESQUILE

■ **BY FOOT:** There is a 0.75-mile trail on the island with a picnic area along the way.

NOTE: No other means of touring the island are available. Canoeists are discouraged from exploring the environs of the island because of strong currents in the river.

WHAT TO SEE

■ **LANDSCAPE AND CLIMATE** The island, 1,329 acres, is shaped like a thumb, 2 miles long and a mile wide, and 20 feet above sea level. Average temperatures range from 100 degrees in summer to 50 degrees in winter. Biting insects abound during the summer. Spring and fall are the best seasons.

■ **PLANT LIFE** About 800 acres of the refuge are wooded bottomland and swamp; there are about 250 acres of tidal marsh. The remainder is agricultural land farmed for crops, cattle, and wildlife food and cover.

Bottomland and swamp Green ash, tulip poplar, sweet gum, and dogwood are the major tree species in these wooded wetlands. The sweet gum, with star-shaped leaves, often grows a conical crown, though sometimes it's domed; in the wild or as an ornamental it is especially lovely in fall when its leaves turn several colors, yellow to deep red.

Marshes The brackish marsh here supports species such as cattail, arrow arum, rice cutgrass, and pickerelweed.

Agricultural land Grasses such as rye, clover, and fescue offer food and cover for numerous bird species. Meadowlarks love this habitat.

■ **ANIMAL LIFE** Since the refuge is relatively undeveloped and does not host crowds of visitors, animals are undisturbed.

Birds A pair of bald eagles has nested here since 1998, and a dozen or so winter here. Ospreys on their nests are visible in spring and summer. Many warblers pass through in fall and spring. Bluebirds are common (especially in meadows); look for the blue-back, red-breast and rust-colored throat. The refuge also has wild turkeys—remember its original name—and bobwhite quail. A few thousand waterfowl winter here.

Mammals White-tailed deer abound. Smaller mammals include red fox, opossums, raccoon and—rejoice if you see one—a few mink. This elusive critter is about 2 feet long, in a dark brown suit with a white spot under his chin; it prowls the shores of waterbodies in search of smaller mammals, fish, birds, and crayfish.

Reptiles and amphibians The refuge has snapping turtles, green snakes, black rat snakes, and fence lizards. One handsome reptile to admire but avoid handling is the copperhead (20 to 50 inches long, copper/orange/pink with chestnut bands on the back), whose bite is painful but rarely life-threatening. Copperheads bask on logs and rocks. Amphibians include green frogs, green tree frogs, and American toads.

HUNTING AND FISHING There are limited deer hunts, by bow and shotgun, in Oct. and Nov. Contact the refuge for more details.

There is no fishing allowed on the refuge.

ACTIVITIES

■ **CAMPING:** No camping is allowed on this refuge.

■ **SWIMMING:** No swimming is allowed on the refuge, because of dangerous currents.

■ **WILDLIFE OBSERVATION:** The footpath passes through most habitats on the island. Along the way, beaver dams and lodges can be seen. Maybe even beavers, if you're here early or late in the day.

■ **PHOTOGRAPHY:** A new observation tower looks out over mudflats, where waterfowl, shorebirds, and bald eagles can be spotted.

■ **PUBLICATIONS:** At the trailhead is a kiosk with pamphlets describing the refuge.

Canaan Valley NWR
Tucker County, West Virginia

Freshwater wetland, Canaan Valley NWR

Mountain valleys are the stuff of dreams and legend, green recesses hiding secret Shangri-las that are realms away from the outside world. Tucked away in the Allegheny Mountains of northeastern West Virginia is one such valley, where the ancient past still lives, by the name of Canaan (pronounced *Ca-nane* by locals).

A visit to Canaan Valley is like a trip back to the Pleistocene Ice Ages, when the Middle Atlantic had a climate similar to that of Canada's boreal forests. In the valley, northern conifers grow among swamps and bogs; in the open, muskegs and wet meadows make the footing soggy. Drained by the storied Blackwater River—its amber waters stained by tannic acid from fallen hemlock and red spruce needles—the valley is 14 miles long, 5 miles wide, and has an average elevation of 3,200 feet. No other valley of its size and altitude exists east of the Rocky Mountains.

The Blackwater River flows languidly through the upper reaches of the valley. It then surges five stories down over falls, its water crashing into a gorge 8 miles long, filled with roaring white water. Drained by the Blackwater and its tributaries, Canaan Valley holds 8,400 acres of wetlands, the largest freshwater wetland area in the central and southern Appalachians.

Even this remote area, in some of the highest and most rugged landscape in the Mountain State, is not safe from the incursion of human activities; conservationists have battled to protect the watershed around the falls from indiscriminate logging, and forestry companies have heeded the appeal. The main threat to the local environment has been affluence, in the form of second-home developments. To help preserve the valley's unusual boreal ecosystem, a National Wildlife Refuge was created here on August 11, 1994. The establishment of the Canaan Valley NWR was a landmark in more ways than one; it became the 500th refuge in the NWR System.

HISTORY

The difficult terrain and climate of the Canaan Valley region were not particularly sought after by Native Americans, although the area was traversed by peoples from surrounding regions, such as the Shawnee and Iroquois. Euro-American settlers began entering the valley in the early 1800s. Logging, mining, and small-scale farming were their mainstays. Today, many residents earn a living in service industries, catering to tourism.

The ecological importance of the valley was recognized in 1974, when the secretary of the interior designated a portion of it as a National Landmark. In 1979, establishment of a refuge there was proposed, but 15 years passed before land was purchased. Canaan Valley NWR now totals about 3,200 acres, not nearly enough to protect the entire valley. However, backed by state agencies and conservation groups, the U.S. Fish & Wildlife Service is attempting to increase land acquisition in what some have called "a living museum of the Ice Age in West Virginia."

GETTING THERE

From the north, take Rte. 219 south to Rte. 32 south, leading to Canaan Valley. From the east, head along Rte. 50 to Rte. 93 to Rte. 32. Either way, headquarters is off Rte. 32, about 9 mi. south of the town of Davis.

■ **SEASON:** Refuge open year-round.
■ **HOURS:** General refuge: sunrise to sunset. Refuge office, weekdays, 7 a.m.–3:30 p.m.
■ **FEES:** None.
■ **ADDRESS:** Canaan Valley NWR, HC70 Box 189, Davis WV 26230
■ **TELEPHONE:** 304/866-3858

TOURING CANAAN VALLEY

■ **BY AUTOMOBILE:** Curtland Road and Freeland Road offer the best opportunities to see the refuge by automobile.
■ **BY FOOT:** There are three short walking trails, two off Old Timberline Road and one off Freeland Road.

WHAT ARE WETLANDS? The name says it all. A wetland is land that is land that is wet—under water—for a period of time, on a regular basis, as opposed to dry land or bodies of water. According to scientific thinking, if land is covered by water for more than two weeks annually or even every other year, and the soil is saturated within one foot of the surface, it is a wetland. Wetlands are an in-between habitat, sometimes under water, sometimes above it. A technical U.S. Fish & Wildlife Service definition puts it this way: "Wetlands are lands transitional between terrestrial and aquatic ecosystems where the water table is usually at or near the surface or the land is covered by shallow water." A wetland can be a marsh, covered by water except in extreme drought. It can be a wet meadow, soggy during the spring. It can be a seasonally flooded wooded swamp, a bog, or an expanse of cordgrass in an estuary. Scientists consider three factors critical to designating a place as a wetland. Obviously, there must be a source of water—from snowmelt, springs, or river overflow, for example. The soil must retain water. And the plants living there are species that can survive when soil oxygen is depleted by flooding, even for a few days. Only a third of the plants growing in the United States can survive this sort of oxygen deficiency.

■ **BY BICYCLE:** Mountain biking is not permitted on the walking trails, but bicycling is welcome on designated access roads.

WHAT TO SEE

■ **LANDSCAPE AND CLIMATE** Canaan Valley lies within the contorted mountains on the eastern edge of the Appalachian Plateau, helter-skelter peaks that end in a high front overlooking the orderly ridge-and-valley chains of the eastern Appalachians. Some mountains in this region surpass 4,000 feet. Along the front, there are 1,000-foot escarpments, and in some places slopes of more than 2,000 feet between summit and valley. The climate is cool and wet, with chilly fogs descending even in summer and frigid temperatures, sometimes well below zero, along with heavy snows (more than 100 inches) common in winter.

■ **PLANT LIFE** Canaan Valley supports more than 40 different plant communities, wetland and upland, with almost 600 species of plants, some at home there since the Pleistocene era. Many of these plants are species that grow more commonly far to the north, in Canada, such as red spruce on slopes above the valley. Within the valley are bogs, wet aspen thickets, and marshes.

■ **ANIMAL LIFE** Almost 300 species of vertebrates have been recorded in Canaan Valley—not an immense number, compared with other refuges, but they include some unusual creatures and large populations of important animals that are dwindling elsewhere.

Birds The wings of the American woodcock whistle in aerial courtship dances during spring. Their long bills probe wet meadows for earthworms. Inland shorebirds, a famed game species, American woodcock have been in a decline. Canaan Valley is a spring and fall migration area for the nationís largest breeding unit of this species. Among other birds occasionally seen in the valley are loggerhead shrike, northern goshawk, sedge wrens, and the rough-legged hawk.

Mammals Roving Canaan Valley are black bear and white-tailed deer. The valley also hosts many small mammals dependent on moist environments, many of them rare outside of this haven. Among these are the southern rock vole, northern water shrew, meadow jumping mouse, and the endangered northern Virginia flying squirrel. Otters and beavers, common here and elsewhere, are frequently seen in the river.

Bobolink

CANAAN VALLEY NWR

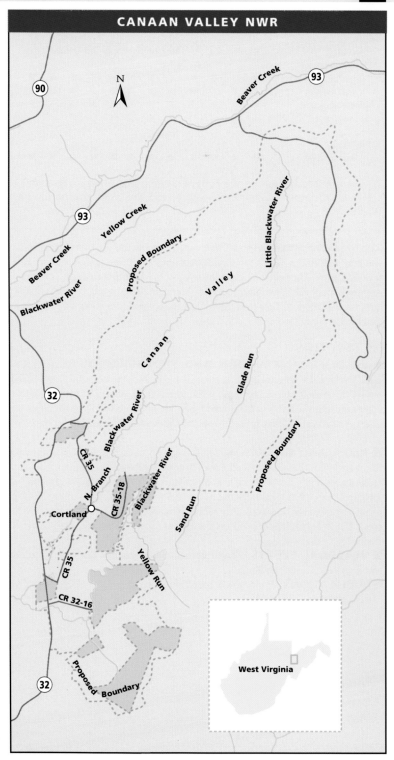

West Virginia

CANAAN VALLEY HUNTING AND FISHING SEASONS

Hunting (Seasons may vary)	Jan	Feb	Mar	Apr	May	Jun	Jul	Aug	Sep	Oct	Nov	Dec
white-tailed deer										■	■	■
wild turkey				■						■		
Canada goose									■			
woodcock										■		
Fishing												
brook trout	■	■	■	■	■	■	■	■	■	■	■	■

For more information on the current hunting and fishing regulations, including license requirements, seasons, and bag limits, consult refuge office.

Reptiles and amphibians Under fallen logs and leaf littler in Canaan Valley, you may well find a 3-inch salamander, coal black with bronze dots on its back, seeking shelter. The valley is one of the few places where this creature, confined to Appalachian pockets, remains. Scurrying about, but circumspect enough that visitors probably will not see it, is the coal skink, a lizard that sometimes heads for water when frightened.

ACTIVITIES

■ **WILDLIFE OBSERVATION AND PHOTOGRAPHY:** From Freeland Trail, explore the meadows for grasslands birds, such as bobolinks and meadowlarks, that can be seen in spring and summer. Wildlife observation opportunities will increase as the refuge is developed. There are no special facilities for photographers. A dozen miles away is Blackwater Falls, the most photographed spot in West Virginia.

■ **HIKES AND WALKS:** The refuge has two main walking trails, Freeland Road and Old Timberline Road (Beall Track). Freeland (0.75 mile round-trip) crosses a field into beaver pond area and winds back through wetlands with balsam firs. Beall offers two trails: the north (2.5 miles round-trip) travels through forest, wet meadow, bogs, and early successional vegetation reverting to forest; the south (1.5 miles round-trip) follows the edge of a forest and passes the Blackwater River.

■ **SEASONAL EVENTS:** May: International Migratory Bird Day; October: National Wildlife Refuge Week.

■ **PUBLICATIONS:** Hunting brochure, refuge fact sheets.

Ohio River Islands NWR
Parkersburg, West Virginia

Ohio River, Ohio River Islands NWR

The Ohio River Islands are the quintessential islands in a stream. They were built of sand, gravel, and boulders deposited by streams and rivulets that flowed from Ice Age glaciers, which stopped just short of the river and began to melt about 12,000 years ago. Because the glacial waters have long since dried up and manipulation of the river for navigation purposes has changed currents, islands like these no longer form. In the words of a scientific study, the Ohio River islands and the scarce wildlife habitats they shelter are "irreplaceable."

HISTORY

In the early 1900s, there were almost 60 of these islands, ranging in length from a few hundred yards to about three miles, strung out along the Ohio River for 362 miles, from just south of Pittsburgh, Pennsylvania, to eastern Kentucky. Today, there are scarcely more than 40. The other islands have vanished, a result of such human activities as dredging for navigation, sand, and gravel; drilling for oil and gas; and recreational use. Six of those that remain are fully developed.

More than 20 of the islands, the bulk of them in West Virginia's share of the river, have been protected by the Ohio River Islands National Wildlife Refuge. They may not be pristine, but, together with the fish and wildlife that find havens among them, they are indeed a trip back in time, to the days when the river was truly wild.

Middens of shells, mostly freshwater mussels, testify that Native Americans used the islands and their fertile fish and game resources since the glacial retreat. In colonial times, George Washington noted the importance of the islands during his survey expeditions to what then was the West. After the American Revolution, a trickle of settlers here turned into a tide. By the middle of the 20th century, the islands, which had withstood the savagery of floods and wilt of drought, were melting away as the glaciers did, not because of nature but because of human interference. To stem the tide of destruction, the U.S. Fish & Wildlife Service purchased eight islands in 1990. Today, the number has almost tripled, preserving more than 2,700 acres of land and underwater habitat.

GETTING THERE

All but two islands are accessible only by boat. However, Middle Island, 2 mi. long and in St. Marys, West Virginia, is reachable by a bridge. You will find the town by taking Rte. 2 north, off I-77. Wheeling Island is in the center of the city of Wheeling, West Virginia. For refuge headquarters, take Rte. 50 east from I-77 into Parkersburg.

■ **SEASON:** Refuge open year-round
■ **HOURS:** General refuge: Sunrise to sunset. Headquarters: 8 a.m.–4:30 p.m., weekdays.
■ **FEES:** None.
■ **ADDRESS:** Ohio River Islands NWR, 3004 7th St., P.O. Box 1811, Parkersburg, WV 26102
■ **TELEPHONE:** 304/422-0752

TOURING OHIO RIVER ISLANDS

■ **BY AUTOMOBILE:** Middle Island has a 1.5-mile auto-tour drive.
■ **BY FOOT:** There is a short hiking trail on Middle Island.
■ **BY BICYCLE:** The auto-tour route is open to bicycles; however, the hiking trail is not.

Chipmunk

■ **BY CANOE, KAYAK, OR BOAT:** The islands are visited most often by boat. The river is heavily trafficked, so be sure to check the refuge for any regulations and safety information. The refuge does not offer boat rentals, but powerboats and pontoon boats are available for rental at Belpre, Ohio, across the river from the refuge.

WHAT TO SEE

■ **LANDSCAPE AND CLIMATE** Cold in winter, relatively hot in summer is the norm for the Ohio River Valley. The surrounding landscape ranges from hilly to rolling. The islands themselves are in a floodplain, flat and rich in alluvial soil. Habitats of primary importance here are underwater beds of gravel and sand, surrounding the islands, and the quiet water between the islands the mainland shore. These river islands shield their backwaters from the rush of the river, offering sheltered waters where aquatic plants grow and fish and wildlife can feed.

■ **PLANT LIFE**
Riverine wetlands The shallows around the islands support beds of rooted aquatic plants: pondweeds and water milfoil, for example. Minnows that feed on plankton and vegetative matter congregate there, as do the largemouth bass and channel catfish that feed upon them.
Moist forests In moist soil forests of silver maple, sycamore, and cottonwood can thrive. Under their shade are herbaceous plants, such as touch-me-not and snakeroot. The seed pods of ripe touch-me-nots burst easily to scatter the seeds of

this member of the impatiens family. These woodlands grow in what are called bottomlands, seasonally flooded and an ecological interface that provides habitat for creatures of the water, such as wood ducks, and those of the forest: raccoons and pileated woodpeckers, to name but two.

■ **ANIMAL LIFE** Seaside refuges of the mid-Atlantic support creatures of water and land. So do the freshwater fringes and interior woods of the Ohio River islands. Perhaps the most important animals of the refuge are those that are enclosed by shells of sculpted calcium carbonate, freshwater mussels that were plentiful foods of Native Americans but are disappearing today because of pollution and such disturbances as dredging, poaching, and the more immediate threat of nonnative zebra mussels.

Birds Nearly 200 species of birds use the islands and their waters. Great blue heron chicks nest, while wood ducks thrive in the bottomlands, feeding on acorns in fall. Warblers use the woodlands as migratory stopovers in spring.

Mammals The presence of so much water determines what mammals can live here. Beaver and muskrat ply the stream, especially in the quiet waters on downstream sides of the islands. White-tailed deer are excellent swimmers. They live and breed on many of the islands. Chipmunks scurry around the ground, feeding on acorns and nuts, and fox squirrels have been seen—believe it or not—swimming across the river.

Fish Boats clustered around the islands tell the story. These waters are the home of more than 50 warm-water fish species, including largemouth bass, white bass, and sauger.

Invertebrates The Ice Age beds of sand and gravel are mini-refuges for freshwater mussels, once so common that they furnished Native Americans with a major portion of their diet, now dwindling. A prize among them, endangered now and rarely found elsewhere, is the pink mucket Visitors are not likely to see these.

HUNTING AND FISHING To hunt on the refuge, you must obtain a special permit (in addition to a state license), available free of charge at the refuge headquarters. There are several hunts throughout the year, in accordance with state seasons: archery, **deer**, **waterfowl**, **rabbit**, and **squirrel**. Contact the refuge for specific dates and more details. Because hunting is allowed only on certain parts of the refuge, it is best to pick up a hunting brochure from the refuge.

Fishing is allowed year-round, under state regulations. Anglers most often find **channel** and **flathead catfish**, **small-** and **largemouth bass**, and **sauger**.

ACTIVITIES

■ **CAMPING:** There is no camping on the refuge; however, there is a campground at the nearby Wayne National Forest, in Marietta, Ohio. You may contact the Forest office at 740/373-9055.

■ **WILDLIFE OBSERVATION AND PHOTOGRAPHY:** Observing wildlife on the Ohio River Islands is a catch-as-catch-can affair. For casual visitors, the trail on Middle Island is probably best. There is a wildlife blind on Middle Island.

■ **PUBLICATIONS:** Refuge brochure (describing the property and activities), refuge hunting brochure.

Appendix

NONVISITABLE NATIONAL WILDLIFE REFUGES

Below is a list of other National Wildlife Refuges in the Mid-Atlantic states. These refuges are not open to the public.

Martin NWR
Martin NWR
Smith Island
Ewell, MD 21824
410/425-4971

Susquehanna NWR
c/o Blackwater NWR
2145 Key Wallace Dr.
Cambridge, MD 21613
410/228-2692

Killcohook Coordination Area
c/o Supawna Meadows NWR
197 Lighthouse Rd.
Pennsville, NJ 08070
609/935-1487

Supawna Meadows NWR
197 Lighthouse Rd.
Pennsville, NJ 08070
609/935-1487

Conscience Point NWR
c/o Long Island NWR Complex
P.O. Box 21
Shirley, NY 11967
516/286-0485

Seatuck NWR
c/o Long Island NWR Complex
P.O. Box 21
Shirley, NY 11967
516/286-0485

Featherstone NWR
c/o Mason Neck NWR
14344 Jefferson Davis Hwy.
Woodbridge, VA 22191-2890
703/690-1297

Fishermans Island NWR
c/o Eastern Shore of Virginia NWR
5003 Hallett Circle
Cape Charles, VA 23310
757/331-2760

Marumsco NWR
c/o Mason Neck NWR
14344 Jefferson Davis Hwy.
Woodbridge, VA 22191-2890
703/690-1297

Nansemond NWR
c/o Great Dismal Swamp NWR
P.O. Box 349
Suffolk, VA 23439-0349
757/986-3705

Plum Tree Island NWR
c/o Back Bay NWR
4005 Sandpiper Rd.
Virginia Beach, VA 23456-2412
757/721-2412

Wallops Island NWR
c/o Chincoteague NWR
Box 62
Chincoteague, VA 23336
757/336-6122

FEDERAL RECREATION FEES

Some—but not all—NWRs and other federal outdoor recreation areas require payment of entrance or use fees (the latter for facilities such as boat ramps). There are several congressionally authorized entrance fee passes:

■ ANNUAL PASSES

Golden Eagle Passport Valid for most national parks, monuments, historic sites, recreation areas and national wildlife refuges. Admits the passport signee and any accompanying passengers in a private vehicle. Good for 12-months. Purchase at any federal area where an entrance fee is charged. The 1999 fee for this pass was $50.00

Federal Duck Stamp Authorized in 1934 as a federal permit to hunt waterfowl and as a source of revenue to purchase wetlands, the Duck Stamp now also serves as an annual entrance pass to NWRs. Admits holder and accompanying passengers in a private vehicle. Good from July 1 for one year. Valid for *entrance* fees only. Purchase at post offices and many NWRs or from Federal Duck Stamp Office, 800/782-6724, or at Wal-Mart, Kmart or other sporting good stores.

■ LIFETIME PASSES

Golden Access Passport Lifetime entrance pass—for persons who are blind or permanently disabled—to most national parks and NWRs. Admits signee and any accompany passengers in a private vehicle. Provides 50% discount on federal use fees charged for facilities and services such as camping, or boating. Must be obtained in person at a federal recreation area charging a fee. Obtain by showing proof of medically determined permanent disability or eligibility for receiving benefits under federal law.

Golden Age Passport Lifetime entrance pass—for persons 62 years of age or older—to national parks and NWRs. Admits signee and any accompanying passengers in a private vehicle. Provides 50% discount on federal use fees charged for facilities and services such as camping, or boating. Must be obtained in person at a federal recreation area charging a fee. One-time $10.00 processing charge. Available only to U.S. citizens or permanent residents.

For more information, contact your local federal recreation area for a copy of the *Federal Recreation Passport Program* brochure.

VOLUNTEER ACTIVITIES

Each year, 30,000 Americans volunteer their time and talents to help the U.S. Fish & Wildlife Service conserve the nation's precious wildlife and their habitats. Volunteers conduct Fish & Wildlife population surveys, lead public tours and other recreational programs, protect endangered species, restore habitat, and run environmental education programs.

The NWR volunteer program is as diverse as are the refuges themselves. There is no "typical" Fish & Wildlife Service volunteer. The different ages, backgrounds, and experiences volunteers bring with them is one of the greatest strengths of the program. Refuge managers also work with their neighbors, conservation groups, colleges and universities, and business organizations.

A growing number of people are taking pride in the stewardship of local national wildlife refuges by organizing non-profit organizations to support individual refuges. These refuge community partner groups, which numbered about 200 in 2000, have been so helpful that the Fish & Wildlife Service, National Audubon Society, National Wildlife Refuge Association, and National Fish & Wildlife Foundation now carry out a national program called the "Refuge System Friends Initiative" to coordinate and strengthen existing partnerships, to jump start new ones, and to organize other efforts promoting community involvement in activities associated with the National Wildlife Refuge System.

For more information on how to get involved, visit the Fish & Wildlife Service Homepage at http://refuges.fws.gov; or contact one of the Volunteer Coordinator offices listed on the U.S. Fish & Wildlife General Information list of addresses below or the U. S. Fish & Wildlife Service, Division of Refuges, Attn: Volunteer Coordinator, 4401 North Fairfax Drive, Arlington, VA 22203; 703/358-2303.

U.S. FISH & WILDLIFE GENERAL INFORMATION

Below is a list of addresses to contact for more inforamation concerning the National Wildlife Refuge System.

U.S. Fish & Wildlife Service
Division of Refuges
4401 North Fairfax Dr., Room 670
Arlington, Virginia 22203
703/358-1744
Web site: fws.refuges.gov

F & W Service Publications:
800/344-WILD

U.S. Fish & Wildlife Service
Pacific Region
911 NE 11th Ave.
Eastside Federal Complex
Portland, OR 97232-4181
External Affairs Office: 503/231-6120
Volunteer Coordinator: 503/231-2077
The Pacific Region office oversees the refuges in California, Hawaii, Idaho, Nevada, Oregon, and Washington.

U.S. Fish & Wildlife Service
Southwest Region
500 Gold Ave., SW
P.O. Box 1306
Albuquerque, NM 87103
External Affairs Office: 505/248-6285
Volunteer Coordinator: 505/248-6635
The Southwest Region office oversees the refuges in Arizona, New Mexico, Oklahoma, and Texas.

U.S. Fish & Wildlife Service
Great Lakes-Big Rivers
Region
1 Federal Dr.
Federal Building
Fort Snelling, MN 55111-4056
External Affairs Office: 612/713-5310
Volunteer Coordinator: 612/713-5444
The Great Lakes-Big Rivers Region office oversees the refuges in Iowa, Illinois, Indiana, Michigan, Minnesota, Missouri, Ohio, and Wisconsin.

U.S. Fish & Wildlife Service
Southeast Region
1875 Century Center Blvd.
Atlanta, GA 30345
External Affairs Office: 404/679-7288
Volunteer Coordinator: 404/679-7178
The Southeast Region office oversees the refuges in Alabama, Arkansas, Florida, Georgia, Kentucky, Lousiana, Mississippi, North Carolina, South Carolina, Tennessee, and Puerto Rico.

U.S. Fish & Wildlife Service
Northeast Region
300 Westgate Center Dr.
Hadley, MA 01035-9589
External Affairs Office: 413/253-8325
Volunteer Coordinator: 413/253-8303
The Northeast Region office oversees the refuges in Connecticut, Delaware, Massachusetts, Maine, New Hampshire, New Jersey, New York, Pennsylvania, Rhode Island, Vermont, Virginia, West Virginia.

U.S. Fish & Wildlife Service
Mountain-Prairie Region
P.O. Box 25486
Denver Federal Center
P. O. Box 25486
Denver, CO 80225
External Affairs Office: 303/236-7905
Volunteer Coordinator: 303/236-8145, x 614
The Mountain-Prairie Region office oversees the refuges in Colorado, Kansas, Montana, Nebraska, North Dakota, South Dakota, Utah, and Wyoming.

U.S. Fish & Wildlife Service
Alaska Region
1011 East Tudor Rd.
Anchorage, AK 99503
External Affairs Office: 907/786-3309
Volunteer Coordinator: 907/786-3391

NATIONAL AUDUBON SOCIETY WILDLIFE SANCTUARIES

National Audubon Society's 100 sanctuaries comprise 150,000 acres and include a wide range of habitats. Audubon managers and scientists use the sanctuaries for rigorous field research and for testing wildlife management strategies. The following is a list of 24 sanctuaries open to the public. Sanctuaries open by appointment only are marked with an asterisk.

EDWARD M. BRIGHAM III ALKALI LAKE SANCTUARY*
c/o North Dakota State Office
118 Broadway, Suite 502
Fargo, ND 58102
701/298-3373

FRANCIS BEIDLER FOREST SANCTUARY
336 Sanctuary Rd.
Harleyville, SC 29448
843/462-2160

BORESTONE MOUNTAIN SANCTUARY
P.O. Box 524
118 Union Square
Dover-Foxcroft, ME 04426
207/564-7946

CLYDE E. BUCKLEY SANCTUARY
1305 Germany Rd.
Frankfort, KY 40601
606/873-5711

BUTTERCUP WILDLIFE SANCTUARY*
c/o New York State Office
200 Trillium Lane
Albany, NY 12203
518/869-9731

CONSTITUTION MARSH SANCTUARY
P.O. Box 174
Cold Spring, NY, 10516
914/265-2601

CORKSCREW SWAMP SANCTUARY
375 Sanctuary Rd. West
Naples, FL 34120
941/348-9151

FLORIDA COASTAL ISLANDS SANCTUARY*
410 Ware Blvd., Suite 702
Tampa, FL 33619
813/623-6826

EDWARD L. & CHARLES E. GILLMOR SANCTUARY*
3868 Marsha Dr.
West Valley City, UT 84120
801/966-0464

KISSIMMEE PRAIRIE SANCTUARY*
100 Riverwoods Circle
Lorida, FL 33857
941/467-8497

MAINE COASTAL ISLANDS SANCTUARIES*
Summer (June–Aug.):
12 Audubon Rd.
Bremen, ME 04551
207/529-5828

MILES WILDLIFE SANCTUARY*
99 West Cornwall Rd.
Sharon, CT 06069
860/364-0048

NORTH CAROLINA COASTAL ISLANDS SANCTUARY*
720 Market St.
Wilmington, NC 28401-4647
910/762-9534

NORTHERN CALIFORNIA SANCTUARIES*
c/o California State Office
555 Audubon Place
Sacramento, CA 95825
916/481-5440

PINE ISLAND SANCTUARY*
P.O. Box 174
Poplar Branch, NC 27965
919/453-2838

RAINEY WILDLIFE SANCTUARY*
10149 Richard Rd.
Abbeville, LA 70510-9216
318/898-5969 (Beeper: leave message)

RESEARCH RANCH SANCTUARY*
HC1, Box 44
Elgin, AZ 85611
520/455-5522

RHEINSTROM HILL WILDLIFE SANCTUARY*
P.O. Box 1
Craryville, NY 12521
518/325-5203

THEODORE ROOSEVELT SANCTUARY
134 Cove Rd.
Oyster Bay, NY 11771
516/922-3200

LILLIAN ANNETTE ROWE SANCTUARY
44450 Elm Island Rd.
Gibbon, NE 68840
308/468-5282

SABAL PALM GROVE SANCTUARY
P.O. Box 5052
Brownsville, TX 78523
956/541-8034

SILVER BLUFF SANCTUARY*
4542 Silver Bluff Rd.
Jackson, SC 29831
803/827-0781

STARR RANCH SANCTUARY*
100 Bell Canyon Rd.
Trabuco Canyon, CA 92678
949/858-0309

TEXAS COASTAL ISLANDS SANCTUARIES
c/o Texas State Office
2525 Wallingwood, Suite 301
Austin, TX 78746
512/306-0225

BIBLIOGRAPHY AND RESOURCES

Aquatic Biology

Morgan, Ann Haven. *Field Book of Ponds and Streams: An Introduction to the Life of Fresh Water,* New York: G.P. Putnam's Sons, 1930.

Ricciuti, Edward R. *The Beachwalker's Guide,* Garden City, N.Y.: Doubleday/Dolphin, 1982.

Birds

Farrand, John, Jr. *The Audubon Society Master Guide to Birding,* three volumes, New York: Alfred A. Knopf, 1983.

Botany

Silberhorn, Gene M. *Tidal Wetland Plants of Virginia,* Educational Series Number 19, Gloucester Point, Va.: Virginia Institute of Marine Science, 1976.

Sutton, Ann and Myron Sutton. *The Audubon Society Nature Guides, Eastern Forests,* New York: Alfred A. Knopf, 1985.

Cultural History

Trigger, Bruce C., Volume Editor. *Handbook of North American Indians, Volume 15, Northeast,* Washington, D.C.: Smithsonian Institution, 1978.

Field Guides

Conan, Roger. *Peterson Field Guide Series: A Field Guide to Reptiles and Amphibians of the United States and Canada East of the 100th Meridian,* Boston: Houghton Mifflin Co., 1958.

Page, Lawrence M. and Brooks M. Burr. *Freshwater Fishes,* Boston: Houghton Mifflin Co., 1991.

Robbins, Chandler S., Bertel Bruun and Herbert Z. Zim. *Birds of North America,* New York: Golden Press, 1983.

Stokes, Donald and Lillian. *Stokes Field Guide to Birds, Eastern Region,* Boston: Little, Brown and Company, 1996.

Whitaker, John O., Jr. *The Audubon Society Field Guide to North American Mammals,* New York: Alfred A. Knopf, 1980.

General

Holing, Dwight, Susanne Methvin, David Rains Wallace, Edward L. Bowen, Ben Davidson, Edward R. Ricciuti, Michele Strutin, Steven Threndyle, Eugene J. Walter, Jr., and Suzanne Winckler. *Nature Travel, a Nature Company Guide,* New York: Time-Life Books, 1995.

Ricciuti, Edward. *The Natural History of North America,* New York: Gallery Books in association with the American Museum of Natural History, 1990.

Geology

Putnam, William C. *Geology,* New York: Oxford University Press, 1964.

Schuberth, Christopher J. *The Geology of New York City and Environs,* Garden City, N.Y.: The Natural History Press, 1968.

Regional Guides

Kulik, Stephen, Pete Salmansohn, Matthew Schmidt and Heidi Welch. *Northeast, Coastal/Northeast, Inland,* New York: Pantheon Books, 1984.

Lawrence, Susannah. *The Audubon Society Field Guides to Natural Places: Mid-Atlantic States, Coastal,* New York: Pantheon Books, 1984.

Lawrence, Susannah and Barbara Gross. *Mid-Atlantic States, Inland,* New York: Pantheon Books, 1984.

GLOSSARY

4WD Four-wheel-drive vehicle. *See also* ATV.

Accidental A bird species seen only rarely in a certain region and whose normal territory is elsewhere. *See also* occasional.

Acre-foot The amount of water required to cover one acre one foot deep.

Alkali sink An alkaline habitat at the bottom of a basin where there is moisture under the surface.

Alluvial Clay, sand, silt, pebbles, and rocks deposited by running water. River floodplains have alluvial deposits, sometimes called alluvial fans, where a stream exits from mountains onto flatland.

Aquifer Underground layer of porous water-bearing sand, rock, or gravel.

Arthropod Invertebrates, including insects, crustaceans, arachnids, and myriapods, with a semitransparent exoskeleton (hard outer structure) and a segmented body, with jointed appendages in articulated pairs.

ATV All-Terrain-Vehicle. *See also* 4WD and ORV.

Barrier island Coastal island produced by wave action and made of sand. Over time the island shifts and changes shape. Barrier islands protect the mainland from storms, tides, and winds.

Basking The habit of certain creatures such as turtles, snakes, or alligators to expose themselves to the pleasant warmth of the sun by resting on logs, rocks, or other relatively dry areas.

Biome A major ecological community such as a marsh or a forest.

Blowout A hollow formed by wind erosion in a prexisting sand dune, often due to vegetation loss.

Bog Wet, spongy ground filled with sphagnum moss and having highly acidic water.

Bottomland Low-elevation alluvial area, close by a river. Sometimes also called bottoms.

Brackish Water that is less salty than sea water; often found in salt marshes, mangrove swamps, estuaries, and lagoons.

Breachway A gap in a barrier beach or island, forming a connection between sea and lagoon.

Bushwhack To hike through territory without established trails.

Cambium In woody plants, a sheath of cells between external bark and internal wood that generates parallel rows of cells to make new tissue, either as secondary growth or cork.

Canopy The highest layer of the forest, consisting of the crowns of the trees.

Carnivore An animal that is primarily flesh-eating. *See also* herbivore and omnivore.

Climax In a stable ecological community, the plants and animals that will successfully continue to live there.

Colonial birds Birds that live in relatively stable colonies, used annually for breeding and nesting.

Competition A social behavior that organizes the sharing of resources such as space, food, and breeding partners when resources are in short supply.

Coniferous Trees that are needle-leaved or scale-leaved; mostly evergreen and cone-bearing, such as pines, spruces, and firs. *See also* deciduous.

Cordgrass Grasses found in marshy areas, capable of growing in brackish waters. Varieties include salt-marsh cordgrass, hay, spike grass, and glasswort.

Crust The outer layer of the earth, between 15 to 40 miles thick.

Crustacean A hard-shelled, usually aquatic, arthropod such as a lobster or crab. *See also* arthropod.

DDT An insecticide ($C14H9Cl5$), toxic to animals and human beings whether ingested or absorbed through skin; particularly devastating to certain bird populations, DDT was generally banned in the U.S. in 1972.

Deciduous Plants that shed or lose their foliage at the conclusion of the growing season, as in "deciduous trees," such as hardwoods (maple, beech, oak, etc.). *See also* coniferous.

Delmarva The peninsula extending along the eastern end of Chesapeake Bay, separating it from the Atlantic Ocean, including portions of three states: Delaware, Maryland, and Virginia.

Delta A triangular alluvial deposit at a river's mouth or at the mouth of a tidal inlet. *See also* alluvial.

Dominant The species most characteristic of a plant or animal community, usually influencing the types and numbers of other species in the same community.

Ecological niche An organism's function, status, or occupied area in its ecological community.

Ecosystem A mostly self-contained community consisting of an environment and the animals and plants that live there.

Emergent plants Plants adapted to living in shallow water or in saturated soils such as marshes or wetlands.

Endangered species A species determined by the federal government to be in danger of extinction throughout all or a significant portion of its range (Endangered Species Act, 1973). *See also* threatened.

Endemic species Species that evolved in a certain place and live naturally nowhere else. *See also* indigenous species.

Epiphyte A type of plant (often found in swamps) that lives on a tree instead of on the soil. Epiphytes are not parasitic; they collect their own water and minerals and perform photosynthesis.

Esker An extended gravel ridge left by a river or stream that runs beneath a decaying glacier.

Estuary The lower part of a river where freshwater meets tidal salt water. Usually characterized by abundant animal and plant life.

Evergreen A tree, shrub, or other plant whose leaves remain green through all seasons.

Exotic A plant or animal not native to the territory. Many exotic plants and animals displace native species.

Extirpation The elimination of a species by unnatural causes, such as overhunting or overfishing.

Fall line A line between the piedmont and the coastal plain below which rivers flow through relatively flat terrain. Large rivers are navigable from the ocean to the fall line.

Fauna Animals, especially those of a certain region or era, generally considered as a group. *See also* flora.

Finger Lakes Eleven long, narrow glacial lakes in central New York State (largest and deepest are Cayuga and Seneca) that were filled with water after the last Ice Age.

Fledge To raise birds until they have their feathers and are able to fly.

Floodplain A low-lying, flat area along a river where flooding is common.

Flora Plants, especially those of a certain region or era, generally considered as a group. *See also* fauna.

Flyway A migratory route, providing food and shelter, followed by large numbers of birds.

Forb Any herb that is not in the grass family; forbs are commonly found in fields, prairies, or meadows.

Frond A fern leaf, a compound palm leaf, or a leaflike thallus (where leaf and stem are continuous), as with seaweed and lichen.

Glacial outwash Sediment dropped by rivers or streams as they flow away from melting glaciers.

Glacial till An unsorted mix of clay, sand, and rock transported and left by glacial action.

Gneiss A common and rather erosion-resistant metamorphic rock originating from shale, characterized by alternating dark and light bands.

Grassy bald A summit area devoid of trees due to shallow or absent soil overlying bedrock (ledge).

Greentree reservoir An area seasonally flooded by opening dikes. Oaks, hickories, and other water-tolerant trees drop nuts (mast) into the water. Migratory birds and other wildlife feed on the mast during winter.

Habitat The area or environment where a plant or animal, or communities of plants or animals, normally live, as in an alpine habitat.

Hammock A fertile spot of high ground in a wetland that supports the growth of hardwood trees.

Hardwoods Flowering trees such as oaks, hickories, maples, and others, as opposed to softwoods and coniferous trees such as pines and hemlocks.

Herbivore An animal that feeds on plant life. *See also* carnivore and omnivore.

Heronry Nesting and breeding site for herons.

Herptiles The class of animals that includes reptiles and amphibians.

Holdfast The attachment, in lieu of roots, that enables seaweed to grip a substrate such as a rock.

Hot spot An opening in the earth's interior from which molten rock erupts, eventually forming a volcano.

Humus Decomposed leaves and other organic material found, for instance, on the forest floor.

Impoundment A man-made body of water controlled by dikes or levees.

Indigenous species Species that arrived unaided by humans but that may also live in other locations.

Inholding Private land surrounded by federal or state lands such as a wildlife refuge.

Intertidal zone The beach or shoreline area located between low and high tide lines.

Introduced species Species brought to a location by humans, intentionally or accidentally; also called nonnative or alien species. *See also* exotic.

Lichen A ground-hugging plant, usually found on rocks, produced by an association between an alga, which manufactures food, and a fungus, which provides support.

Loess Deep, fertile, and loamy soil deposited by wind, the deepest deposits reaching 200 feet.

Magma Underground molten rock.

Management area A section of land within a federal wildlife preserve or forest where specific wildlife management practices are implemented and studied.

Maritime forest Woodland growing near the oceanfront, usually behind dunes, often stunted and composed of pines and oaks.

Marsh A low-elevation transitional area between water (the sea) and land, dominated by grasses in soft, wet soils.

Mast   A general word for nuts, acorns, and other food for wildlife produced by trees in the fall.

Meander   The windings of a stream, river, or path.

Mesozoic   A geologic era, 230-65 million years ago, during which dinosaurs appeared and became extinct, and birds and flowering plants first appeared.

Midden   An accumulation of organic material near a village or dwelling; also called a shell mound.

Migrant   An animal that moves from one habitat to another, as opposed to resident species that live permanently in the same habitat.

Mitigation   The act of creating or enlarging refuges or awarding them water rights to replace wildlife habitat lost because of the damming or channelization of rivers or the building of roads.

Moist-soil unit   A wet area that sprouts annual plants, which attract waterfowl. Naturally produced by river flooding, moist-soil units are artificially created through controlled watering.

Moraine   A formation of rock and soil debris transported and dropped by a glacier.

Neotropical   New world tropics, generally referring to central and northern South America, as in *neotropical* birds.

Nesting species   Birds that take up permanent residence in a habitat.

Occasional   A bird species seen only occasionally in a certain region and whose normal territory is elsewhere.

Oceanic trench   The place where a sinking tectonic plate bends down, creating a declivity in the ocean floor.

Old field   A field that was once cultivated for crops but has been left to grow back into forest.

Old-growth forest   A forest characterized by large trees and a stable ecosystem. Old-growth forests are similar to precolonial forests.

Omnivore   An animal that feeds on both plant and animal material. *See also* carnivore and herbivore.

ORVs   Off-Road-Vehicles. *See also* 4WD and ATV.

Oxbow   A curved section of water (once a bend in a river) that was severed from the river when the river changed course. An oxbow lake is formed by the changing course of a river as it meanders through its floodplain.

Passerine   A bird in the *Passeriformes* order, primarily composed of perching birds and songbirds.

Peat   An accumulation of sphagnum moss and other organic material in wetland areas, known as peat bogs.

Petroglyph   Carving or inscription on a rock.

Photosynthesis   The process by which green plants use the energy in sunlight to create carbohydrates from carbon dioxide and water, generally releasing oxygen as a byproduct.

Pictograph   Pictures painted on rock by indigenous people.

Piedmont   Hilly country between mid-Atlantic coastal plain and the Appalachian Mountains.

Pine Barrens   Sandy-soiled areas with scrubby pines and small oaks, typical of coastal mid-Atlantic region. Term most frequently applied to pine forests in southern half of New Jersey.

Pit and mound topography   Terrain characteristic of damp hemlock woods where shallow-rooted fallen trees create pits (former locations of trees) and mounds (upended root balls).

Plant community Plants and animals that interact in a similar environment within a region.

Pleistocene A geologic era, 1.8 million to 10,000 years ago, known as the great age of glaciers.

Prairie An expansive, undulating, or flat grassland, usually without trees, generally on the plains of mid-continent North America. In the southeast, "prairie" refers to wet grasslands with standing water much of the year.

Prescribed burn A fire that is intentionally set to reduce the buildup of dry organic matter in a forest or grassland, to prevent catastrophic fires later on or to assist plant species whose seeds need intense heat to open.

Proclamation area An area of open water beside or around a coastal refuge where waterfowl are protected from hunting.

Rain shadow An area sheltered from heavy rainfall by mountains that, at their higher altitudes, have drawn much of the rain from the atmosphere.

Raptor A bird of prey with a sharp curved beak and hooked talons. Raptors include hawks, eagles, owls, falcons, and ospreys.

Rhizome A horizontal plant stem, often thick with reserved food material, from which grow shoots above and roots below.

Riparian The bank and associated plant life zone of any water body, including tidewaters.

Riverine Living or located on the banks of a river.

Rookery A nesting place for a colony of birds or other animals (seals, penguins, others).

Salt marsh An expanse of tall grass, usually cordgrass and sedges, located in sheltered places such as the land side of coastal barrier islands or along river mouths and deltas at the sea.

Salt pan A shallow pool of saline water formed by tidal action that usually provides abundant food for plovers, sandpipers, and other wading birds.

Scat Animal fecal droppings.

Scrub A dry area of sandy or otherwise poor soil that supports species adapted to such conditions, such as sand myrtle and prickly pear cactus, or dwarf forms of other species, such as oaks and palmettos.

Sea stack A small, steep-sided rock island lying off the coast.

Second growth Trees in a forest that grow naturally after the original stand is cut or burned. *See also* old growth.

Seeps Small springs that may dry up periodically.

Shorebird A bird, such as a plover or sandpiper, frequently found on or near the seashore.

Shrub-steppe Desertlike lands dominated by sagebrush, tumbleweed, and other dry-weather-adapted plants.

Slough A backwater or creek in a marshy area; sloughs sometimes dry into deep mud.

Spit A narrow point of land, often of sand or gravel, extending into the water.

Staging area A place where birds rest, gather strength, and prepare for the next stage of a journey.

Successional Referring to a series of different plants that establish themselves by territories, from water's edge to drier ground. Also, the series of differing plants that reestablish themselves over time after a fire or the retreat of a glacier.

Sump A pit or reservoir used as a drain or receptacle for liquids.

Swale A low-lying, wet area of land.

Swamp A spongy wetland supporting trees and shrubs (as opposed to a marsh, which is characterized by grasses). Swamps provide habitat for birds, turtles, alligators, and bears and serve as refuges for species extirpated elsewhere. *See also* extirpated.

Tannic acid A brownish acidic substance released by peat and conifers, such as hemlocks and pines.

Test The hard, round exoskeleton of a sea urchin.

Threatened species A species of plant or animal in which population numbers are declining, but not in immediate danger of extinction. Threatened species are protected under the Endangered Species Act of 1973. *See also* endangered.

Tuber A short, underground stem with buds from which new shoots grow.

Understory Plants growing under the canopy of a forest. *See also* canopy.

Vascular plant A fern or another seed-bearing plant with a series of channels for conveying nutrients.

Vernal pool Shallow ponds that fill with spring ("vernal") rains or snowmelt and dry up as summer approaches; temporary homes to certain amphibians.

Wader A long-legged bird, such as a crane or stork, usually found feeding in shallow water.

Wetland A low, moist area, often marsh or swamp, especially when regarded as the natural habitat of wildlife.

Wilderness Area An area of land (within a national forest, national park, or national wildlife refuge) protected under the 1964 Federal Wilderness Act. Logging, construction, and use of mechanized vehicles or tools are prohibited here, and habitats are left in their pristine states. Designated Wilderness is the highest form of federal land protection.

Wrack line Plant, animal, and unnatural debris left on the upper beach by a receding tide.

ACKNOWLEDGMENTS

The pride that national wildlife refuge personnel have in the lands and wildlife under their care was evident to me while I was researching this book. These are busy people, many of whom wear several hats—those of biologist, educator, and administrator, for instance. Yet, they were never too busy to assist me with thorough enthusiasm. Refuge manager or young intern, each and every one of them manifested utmost zeal for their mission—conserving our natural heritage. And they realized that a book such as this could work toward that end. They represent the finest traditions of public service.

—Ed Ricciuti

ABOUT THE AUTHOR

Former Curator of Publications, New York Zoological Society, Edward Ricciuti has written more than 60 books and scores of articles for adults and young people, primarily on nature and science topics, with assignments taking him around the world.

PHOTOGRAPHY CREDITS

We would like to thank the U. S. Fish & Wildlife Service for letting us publish photos from their collection, as well as the other contributing photographers for their wonderful imagery. The pages on which the photos appear are listed after each contributor.

Daniel B. Gibson: 5
John & Karen Hollingsworth: 4, 6, 14, 19, 22, 25, 26, 33, 37, 68, 75, 82, 92, 95, 99, 104, 106, 107, 111, 118, 125, 129, 137, 142
Gary Kramer: xiv, 7, 8, 21, 34, 43, 44, 49, 61, 64, 70, 85, 90, 96, 122, 131, 134
Omni-Photo Communications: iv–v, 30, 58, 72, 78, 120
U.S. Fish & Wildlife Service: 20, 39, 46, 50, 52, 56, 83, 88, 100, 103, 112, 116, 130, 140, 145

NATIONAL AUDUBON SOCIETY
Mission Statement

The mission of National Audubon Society, founded in 1905, is to conserve and restore natural ecosystems, focusing on birds, other wildlife, and their habitats for the benefit of humanity and the earthís biological diversity.

One of the largest, most effective environmental organizations, Audubon has more than 560,000 members, numerous state offices and nature centers, and 500+ chapters in the United States and Latin America, plus a professional staff of scientists, lobbyists, lawyers, policy analysts, and educators. Through our nationwide sanctuary system we manage 150,000 acres of critical wildlife habitat and unique natural areas for birds, wild animals, and rare plant life.

Our award-winning Audubon magazine, published six times a year and sent to all members, carries outstanding articles and color photography on wildlife and nature, and presents in-depth reports on critical environmental issues, as well as conservation news and commentary. We also publish Field Notes, a journal reporting on seasonal bird sightings continent-wide, and Audubon Adventures, a bimonthly childrenís newsletter reaching 500,000 students. Through our ecology camps and workshops in Maine, Connecticut, and Wyoming, we offer professional development for educators and activists; through Audubon Expedition Institute in Belfast, Maine, we offer unique, traveling undergraduate and graduate degree programs in Environmental Education.

Our acclaimed World of Audubon television documentaries on TBS deal with a variety of environmental themes, and our children's series for the Disney Channel, Audubon's Animal Adventures, introduces family audiences to endangered wildlife species. Other Audubon film and television projects include conservation-oriented movies, electronic field trips, and educational videos. National Audubon Society also sponsors books and interactive programs on nature, plus travel programs to exotic places like Antarctica, Africa, Australia, Baja California, Galapagos Islands, Indonesia, and Patagonia.

For information about how you can become an Audubon member, subscribe to Audubon Adventures, or learn more about our camps and workshops, please write or call:

National Audubon Society
Membership Dept.
700 Broadway
New York, New York 10003
212/979-3000
http://www.audubon.org/audubon

JOIN THE NATIONAL AUDUBON SOCIETY—RISK FREE!

Please send me my first issue of AUDUBON magazine and enroll me as a temporary member of the National Audubon Society at the $20 introductory rate—$15 off the regular rate. If I wish to continue as a member, I'll pay your bill when it arrives. If not, I'll return it marked "cancel," owe nothing, and keep the first issue free.

____ Payment Enclosed   ____ Bill Me

Name _____

Street _____

City _____

State/zip _____

Please make checks payable to the National Audubon Society. Allow 4–6 weeks for delivery of magazine. $10 of dues is for AUDUBON magazine. Basic membership, dues are $35.

Mail to:

> NATIONAL AUDUBON SOCIETY
> Membership Data Center
> PO Box 52529
> Boulder, CO 80322-2529